WH

GOD

AND

MEDICINE MEET

Also by Neale Donald Walsch

Conversations with God, Book 1
Conversations with God, Book 1 Guidebook
Conversations with God, Book 2
Meditations from Conversations with God, Book 2
Conversations with God, Book 3
Questions and Answers from Conversations with God
Bringers of the Light
ReCreating Your Self
Conversations with God Re-MIND-er Cards
Moments of Grace
The Wedding Vows from Conversations with God
Neale Donald Walsch on Abundance and Right Livelihood
Neale Donald Walsch on Holistic Living
Neale Donald Walsch on Relationships
Conversations with God for Teens
Friendship with God
Communion with God
Tomorrow's God: Our Greatest Spiritual Challenge
The Little Soul and the Sun
The Little Soul and the Earth
The Complete Conversations with God
Home with God: In a Life that Never Ends
Happier Than God
When Everything Changes, Change Everything
The New Revelations: A Conversation with God
What God Wants: A Compelling Answer to Humanity's Biggest Question
What God Said: The 25 Core Messages of Conversations with God
That Will Change Your Life and the World
The Storm Before the Calm
The Only Thing That Matters
God's Message to the World: You've Got Me All Wrong
Conversations with God for Parents

WHERE
GOD
AND
MEDICINE
MEET

A conversation between a doctor
and a spiritual messenger

NEALE DONALD WALSCH
and BRIT COOPER, M.D.

RAINBOW RIDGE
BOOKS

Cover and interior design by Frame25 Productions
Cover photo © mutlu c/o Shutterstock.com

Published by:
Rainbow Ridge Books, LLC
140 Rainbow Ridge Road
Faber, Virginia 22938
www.rainbowridgebooks.com
434-361-1723

If you are unable to order this book from your local
bookseller, you may order directly from the distributor.

Square One Publishers, Inc.
115 Herricks Road
Garden City Park, NY 11040
Phone: (516) 535-2010
Fax: (516) 535-2014
Toll-free: 877-900-BOOK

Visit the author at:
www.nealedonaldwalsch.com

Library of Congress Cataloging-in-Publication Data applied for.

ISBN 978-1-937907-48-8

10 9 8 7 6 5 4 3 2 1

Printed on acid-free paper in Canada

To Jennifer Jones.
Thank you for your unbending support
in the writing of this book.

To Em Claire.
Neale's life partner, and
the best friend he has ever had.

Authors' Note

The text that follows is a transcription of phone conversations between Brit Cooper, M.D. and spiritual messenger Neale Donald Walsch. Dr. Cooper's voice appears in this Times Roman typeface, and Neale Donald Walsch's voice appears in a sans serif typeface.

Before delving into specific medical topics, we explore the Four Fundamental Questions of Life, which lay the groundwork and set the context for the remainder of the book.

Note also that the word "God" is used throughout this book. The authors understand this term to be synonymous with Life Force, Life Energy, Source, Universe, or, quite simply, Life Itself.

Table of Contents

Foreword

Are medical miracles real and is there a spiritual reason they occur? Is there a place for euthanasia in the mind of the spiritual seeker? Can participating in open-heart surgery and dissecting cadavers tell a medical student anything about the soul? Is there an intersection between spirituality and physicality where the two become one?

Let's get more direct with our questions.

Is there a place for God in the system of modern Western medicine? Should metaphysical/spiritual principles be part of the medical school curriculum? Is keeping patients alive an appropriate top priority for doctors?

The answer to all of the above questions is yes.

It's time we take a look at all this, don't you think? From a new point of view, I mean. From the standpoint of contemporary spirituality. From a place outside the box of our past, and even some of our current, thinking. It's time, yes?

Yes.

So I got on the telephone at the request of a young doctor from Canada (it was all her idea, and I'm glad she had it) and talked with her in weekly conversations over a period of several months to explore Where God and Medicine Meet.

That's the title of a book she said she urgently desired to write as a result of what she said were two highly meaningful and deeply impacting experiences in her life: her movement through, and graduation from, medical school, and her attendance at nine Spiritual Renewal Intensives—5-day retreats which I facilitated over the final two years of her medical training.

Her medical school curriculum had as its foundation the traditional model of Western Medicine. My retreats, on the other hand, were based on a very non-traditional (to put it mildly) spiritual model explored in the *Conversations with God* series of books. Thus, over a period of the same 24 months, now Dr. Brit Cooper (she graduated from the University of British Columbia Medical School in the Class of 2015) found herself continually confronting the crossroads of spirituality and physicality, engaging both aspects of the human encounter with life in a way that few others might ever experience.

When I first met Dr. Cooper as she attended a *CwG* retreat in June of 2013, I experienced her as a remarkably articulate, highly intelligent young woman of 22, who I learned was the youngest member of her medical school class, following undergraduate studies in math and science at the University of Victoria. It was a delight to have her in the room.

I was happily surprised to see her at our very next retreat several months later, and knew then that something she had heard and experienced in relationship to her spiritual life had struck a deep chord within her. I did not, however, expect to see her at seven more *CwG* retreats, and to emerge as one of our most empowering global spokespersons, having then attended, just after earning her M.D. degree, our *CwG* School for Messengers.

Brit had become one of the most energetic and purely motivated students of *Conversations with God* that I have encountered in 20 years of sharing its spiritually revolutionary concepts. So when she asked me if we might produce a book together on the nexus between God and Medicine—a topic that she felt definitely needed exploring, given her medical school experience—I immediately agreed.

I knew this would be a text of immediate interest not only to those in ministries and medicine, but to all the people they served. I couldn't imagine anything more fascinating—or vital to the human family.

Thank you for visiting this dialogue with amazing Dr. Brit Cooper and myself. We would both be interested in, and grateful for, your response. Please feel free to join in the dialogue at *www.GodandMedicine.info*

Neale Donald Walsch
Ashland, Oregon

Part One

—

A NEW DIALOGUE ON HEALTH, WELLNESS, AND SPIRITUALITY

Chapter One

THE DIALOGUE BEGINS:
Who Are We Really?

DR. COOPER: I have found one of the most powerful inquiries of the *Conversations with God* material to be the *Four Fundamental Questions of Life:*

1. Who am I?

2. Where am I?

3. Why am I where I am?

4. What do I intend to do about that?

It was the answering of these questions that catapulted my under-standing from being merely conceptual to *transformative.* The material began to have a noticeable impact on my day-to-day life. I began to walk through the world in a brand new way, almost as if my glasses had been cleaned and I could at last see the world through clear lenses. That is, *through the lenses of what is really going on and what we're really "up to" on the planet, and on this journey of being human.*

So I would love to chat about this today, Neale.

I think it's a powerful place to start.

NEALE: Great. There are really *seven* simple questions about Life that I think are important for people to ask themselves . . . yet my observation is that 98 percent of the world's people have never asked themselves those questions. Most go from birth to death, actually, and never even *consider* asking themselves those questions. The questions never even occur to them, except, perhaps, in the most fleeting, passing way—if at all. I have categorized these seven simple questions as: (A) the Three Persistent Questions, and (B) the Four Fundamental Questions of Life.

The first three questions are important because they *contextualize,* or provide a *reason,* for asking the next four. Or, to put it another way, if everything was beautiful and wonderful on the Earth, and the people of this planet were both collectively and individually experiencing the lives that they wished and had hoped to experience, then the Four Fundamental Questions would almost be needless. There would be no real purpose in asking them, and certainly no urgency around the answers.

What *creates* an urgency around the Four Fundamental Questions of Life are the three questions that precede them in my list of Seven Simple Questions. The first question is:

How is it possible for over seven billion people on the Earth to all say they want the same thing and to be unable to get it? That's the contextual basis for the Four Fundamental Questions of Life. As I said, if everyone was living the life they wish they could experience, there would be no point in asking those final four questions.

The only reason to even get into self-examination is not for the spiritual or intellectual exercise of it, but because *something is not working*.

One doesn't walk into a room where the lights are all on and say, "Do you think we should check the fuse box?" Everyone would say, "Why bother? Everything is working fine." *But if you walk into the kitchen and the lights aren't on and the toaster doesn't work and nothing else is operating, you'd better check the breaker box.*

So the Three Persistent Questions are not unimportant. That first question again: How in the world is it possible for 7.3 billion people on this planet to all say, including you and me and all the rest of us, that we all want the same thing, but are unable to get it, except for the tiniest percentage of us?

The second question: Is it possible that there is something we don't fully understand about God and about Life, the understanding of which could change everything?

And the third question: Is it possible there is something we don't understand about *ourselves*, the understanding of which would change how we experience ourselves, and how we relate to all of Life?

DR. COOPER: It's a mind-boggling concept that over seven billion people could all claim to want the same things—peace, love, opportunity, joy, abundance—and be utterly unable to achieve it. I'd never quite thought of it in those terms before.

It certainly puts the truth right in front of our eyes, when it comes to examining the state of our world. And to pondering how a presumably intelligent species—one that can send man to the moon, uncover the mysteries of our ever-expanding universe, unlock the genetic code, and discover miraculous medical miracles—could find itself at such a seeming "impasse" when it comes to the basics of life. Simple things like joy, love, food, and shelter.

And not only do we seem incapable of experiencing these things to the degree that we would like to, we seem to struggle to experience them *in even the smallest degree.*

Speaking of eye-opening things, it certainly wakes us up to the state of the world reading the statistics in your book *God's Message To The World: You've Got Me All Wrong*. To quote from it, over 650 children die per hour of starvation. Almost 21 million women and children are bought and sold into commercial sexual servitude every year. About 2.6 billion are without basic sanitation, and 1.6 without electricity. And the list goes on. So it certainly provides the context for self-examination, both individually and collectively, for all of humanity.

NEALE: And 1.5 billion do not even have access to clean water. Imagine that.

DR. COOPER: It's unbelievable. And Neale, I really want to ask you, *Why?* How is it possible that such circumstances could be "accepted" in our world, almost without a second thought? *Are people not shocked that such a phenomenon is possible?*

NEALE: People live in a bubble. Especially, and probably primarily, people who "have it good." Which is just about 5-to-8 percent of the world's people.

They live in a bubble. They think that because they have it good, everybody has it good. Because they're doing well, everybody's doing well. It doesn't even *occur to them*—it's not even a part of our thinking—that billions of people might not even have access to clean water. Or, that billions of people—not a few hundred thousand, or even a few million, in outlying areas, but billions around the world—need to relieve themselves out-of-doors. It doesn't seem feasible or possible, because it's simply not part of our experience, and it's hard for us to imagine that this is even going on; that any race of compassionate sentient beings would *allow* it to go on.

I spent some time in the Seventies in Central West Africa, and in South America as well, and in other places on the planet where what I'm saying to you is—or at least it was in 1976—the way things are. *It was just how things were.* I visited families in places like Ouagadougou and other locations in Africa where such conditions were rather common.

DR. COOPER: How did it feel to see that?

NEALE: You know, it changed my whole point of view about Life.

I never again allowed myself to become upset or furious because I couldn't get a long-distance phone call through from Los Angeles to New York in seven seconds, and I wanted to know the reason why. I can remember those days when I was so impatient that the modern conveniences of life were not functioning properly for me. You know, "Waiter, waiter!", or whatever. That kind of an attitude.

When I came back from spending two and a half months in Central West Africa, I never again held those attitudes.

I remember being in a so-called hotel in Upper Volta (now known as Burkina Faso) that was actually just a brick shell of a building without any windows. They simply had knockout holes in the wall for windows. If you didn't have a sleeping net—and I did not—you were attacked by mosquitoes, and woke up the next morning with your face swollen. I had to be given medical care at the American Embassy, with all sorts of shots to counteract the effect of being hit with fifty or sixty mosquito bites.

And we're talking about mosquitoes the size of a Volkswagen. Very large creatures.

And in Upper Volta I recall I wanted to call back to the United States. I went to the front desk to ask if there was a lobby phone I could use to call home. (There was no phone in my room.) They said, "Yes, sir, but you'll have to request a long-distance line—and there's a queue, so you'll have to get in the queue."

I had to wait three-and-a-half hours to get a line to the United States, and I was given fifteen minutes to use the line! I recall that vividly—that you had to wait in line and then they would call your name. "Mr. Walsch, your line is available now." And you'd rush to the phone in the lobby and pick it up, and you'd be able to make your call to the United States.

I recall, when I came back to the U.S., thinking of how many times I'd tapped the phone impatiently (this was way before the appearance of cell phones the size of a playing card), and I'd be demanding, "Operator, operator!", wanting to know why I couldn't get a trans-continental call across the country in the blink of an eye.

So I came back from Central West Africa with an acute awareness of *all* that I had been taking for granted—not just the telephone service. And that was a great deal. Not a little bit, but a *great deal.*

I recall going to the home of a family living on the outskirts of Ouagadougou—way outside of town. I traveled there by taxi when I was invited as their guest. They wanted me to visit their home. And it was considered to be a really modern home, because in this home there was *electricity*. The source: One bare bulb hanging on a cord from the ceiling in the main room of the house.

They would take out the bulb during the day and put in an electrical adapter so you could plug an iron, or some other kind of appliance, into it. And in the evening you didn't use appliances, because a bulb was put in there. That was their source of light in this small adobe kind of home, in which lived probably twelve or thirteen people. It was a four-room dwelling.

There was, of course, no indoor plumbing, no shower, no washer-and-dryer, none of those things.

I've been to 26 nations around the world and I can tell you that it's astonishing how many people live without what you and I consider standard, ordinary, every-day conditions that turn out to be quite luxurious to somebody in Ouagadougou.

I would think that the average person, upon seeing that, would then create a context within which they would begin to examine their own life—and life in general. More broadly, life in general.

What's going *on* around the Earth? Why is it this way? What is really happening here?

How is it possible for all of us to say we want the same thing, and we're supposed to be an evolving species . . . how can seven billion members of an evolving species be unable to produce the outcomes we say we want, except for the tiniest percentage of us? Not that the outcomes are, necessarily, washer-and-dryer . . . but surely, just a source of pure drinking water . . .

What is the missing data?

What is it we don't understand?

And that's what led me to clarity about the final Four Fundamental Questions of Life.

DR. COOPER: And what shocks me even more is that, even among the 5 percent of people who hold or control 95 percent of the world's wealth, there is an underlying yet highly prevalent level of discontent and dissatisfaction. *Even those who appear to "have it good" are not guaranteed to have an underlying level of happiness, in the way we might expect.*

I recall you saying in your book *God's Message To The World: You've Got Me All Wrong* that when even the "best off" members of a species are unhappy, it's a sure sign that something is amiss. It's a sure sign that there is *missing data* of some sort. That we are lacking clarity on why we are here, what we are "up to," and what we are trying to achieve—both individually and collectively—such that the joy and happiness that is the birthright of every human being almost becomes elusive, seemingly impossible to achieve, and always just out of reach.

Further to that, I have noticed working in the medical profession that the rates of mental health crises have skyrocketed over the past several years, in a way that cannot be explained by biology and medicine alone. This further raises my suspicion that there is something we may not fully understand about life and about ourselves, *the understanding of which would change everything.*

NEALE: You're right—when even the best off of us are lacking in happiness and fulfillment, that's a sure sign that something is amiss.

DR. COOPER: It is!

And those "luxuries" you mention us taking for granted are more often than not viewed as *hassles* in the modern-day world. It's a "hassle" to make a long-distance phone call, a "hassle" to drive through traffic, and a "hassle" to get groceries and cook meals, *when others would be indescribably grateful just to get the leftovers we throw in the garbage.*

Clearly, there is something that does not add up in this picture. And clearly, the conditions around us do merit further investigation.

NEALE: And the conditions around us have nothing to do with whether we're happy or not happy. We just think that they do. But it turns out it's not about the car in the driveway, or the house.

You know, I sometimes wince when I hear myself and my contemporaries talk about the things that we find intolerable, like driving through traffic. Some people find it intolerable—can you imagine this, an *intolerable condition*—that they have to drag the vacuum cleaner from the first floor to the second floor to clean the carpets once a week.

So people now have to have a vacuum cleaner on every floor of the house. One for the first floor and one for the second floor—and if you live in a tri-level, one for the third floor—so that you don't have to drag the vacuum cleaner up and down the stairs. God forbid you would have to do that. So we have homes in North America and elsewhere in Europe (and in other places in the western world) where in fact, just to make a point of it, there are two, and sometimes *three*, vacuum cleaners in one house.

I call that the Vacuum-Cleaner Syndrome.

DR. COOPER: *Good diagnosis there.* And yes, I agree with you. It's not the external circumstances of our lives that determine our happiness. But I think it is our mistaken assumption that these circumstances *define Who We Are.* In this regard, we have *forgotten Who We Really Are.*

So this takes us to the first of the Four Fundamental Questions of Life, *Who am I?*

I think the vast majority of the world, including myself before I met you, would be tempted to define themselves by listing things, such as their education, their career, their families, their friends, their hobbies, their possessions, and their accomplishments. In this, we mistake "who we are" with the "story of our lives"—*and the two are not the same.*

The "story of our lives" tells people what we have done and the road we have travelled, but it says nothing about the fundamental essence of Who We Are. It fails to address the *spiritual component,* which I have come to understand is the most important aspect of all.

In my observation, the happiness that comes from connecting with the spiritual piece in ourselves far exceeds anything that could be achieved in the physical realm alone. In other words, the "story of your life," no matter how "good" it gets—even if you're among the 5 percent of the richest people in the world—never can and never will measure up to the truth of Who You Really Are.

So I would venture to say that a true willingness to answer the question *Who am I?*, without relying on your "story" for the answer, is the first step toward true fulfillment in any circumstance.

NEALE: Not only to *answer* the question *Who am I?*, but to *create* the answer.

I wanted to double back just a second here to talk about this business of happiness without three vacuum cleaners in the house, and what I didn't say a moment ago about the people of Ouagadougou is that they were the happiest people I'd ever met in my life.

The evening that I spent in their home—that adobe, or hardened mud brick building, with no windows and one hanging cord for their source of electricity, in which ten or twelve people lived, as I recall—was a revelation. These were the happiest people I'd ever encountered.

They sang and they danced, and they hugged and kissed each other, they enjoyed eating meals together, and the laughter that filled that dwelling was heard all over the place. And I thought, *Oh, my goodness, my heavens, what is it that these people know that I, with my two vacuum cleaners, have only begun to touch? What is it that I don't understand, that they clearly understand?*

And, of course, they clearly understood that their personal happiness had nothing to do with their possessions, or virtually anything material in their lives. It had to do with immaterial things. Things that were not necessarily physical, but the non-physical aspects of their life, which I would characterize, among other things, as simple love. They just loved each other enormously, and they realized that they were all part of the same unit, the same tribe, and the same experience.

So yes, when we have a willingness to ask that first question, *Who Am I?*, and then to *create the answer*, it is immensely powerful to not simply respond to the question intellectually, as an intellectual excursion, but to *create a response that makes sense to our soul.* A response that announces Who We Choose To Be, as opposed to who we imagine ourselves to be.

Who I choose to be is an Individuation of Divinity, a wave on the Ocean of God.

DR. COOPER: I have a question for you. Why do you think it is that so many people in our culture here in North America have such a struggle with that? With embracing a spiritual answer to the question *Who am I?*

Because I've noticed in coming to your retreats, for instance, that many people will resonate with the messages you share. They will go home on a "workshop high," feeling like at last they understand life, and have clarity about who they are and why they're here.

Yet within a few days, or a few weeks, or a few months if they're lucky, many if not most people will revert back to the cultural story that "Who I Am is what I have." And I say this because I work with these people; I get emails from them asking why it's such a challenge to implement these concepts in an ongoing way . . .

So my question is *why?*

NEALE: Because people are reluctant to even consider the possibility of giving up what they have in order to be Who They Really Are. They've confused the experience of their possessions with that which they imagine is prohibiting them from being Who They Are.

People who understand that they can be Who They Are and still be the richest person on Earth, that they can be Who They Really Are and still have three vacuum cleaners, and that being Who You Are does not mean have to give up what you have, are people who stay within their spiritual awareness long after the retreat ends.

But the reason that so many people have a difficult time embracing that notion, and they go back to their Monday through Friday lives, is that they have it in their mind that "Oh, it's all very well and good what Neale is talking about, but you know, I'm not really willing yet, I'm not even sure that I'm able, I don't know how to exist without my stuff. Gosh, just take my iPhone away from me and I'm dead, much less strip me of my laptop. I can't get through the day without my laptop!" And, one could add in many cases, "the other possessions that I have in my life."

And it's understandable that we would be reluctant to do that, even afraid to do that, because we have not been trained. We don't know how to exist without these things!

You know, when I was a youngster I could rattle off the phone numbers of everybody important in my life. My Grandma, my aunt Irene, my friends—I even knew the phone number of the school. These days you ask somebody, "What's the phone number of your cousin Jean?" and they have to look in their cell phone, because we've forgotten how to use our minds to memorize anything.

Watch the younger clerks operating the cash register at the supermarket. If the cash register doesn't tell them how much change the customer has coming, they don't know how to figure it out. They don't know *how to make change.*

When I was a kid, there was no cash register that explained that if you were given a $20 bill and the customer spent $5.37, what they got in change was $14.63. You simply counted backwards, and you learned how to do that pretty quickly. These days, many a nineteen-year-old cashier at the grocery store would be flummoxed at having to stand there and simply make change if they didn't have the machines that tell them exactly how much is owed the customer.

What we've seen in our world is the dumbing down of humanity. And the incapacitation of humanity.

We have seen ourselves *incapacitated.* That is, *we don't know how to survive without these things.*

So naturally, when you get home after a workshop "high," you fall back into your modes of living, because it's self-survival time. We actually don't know how to survive without, you know, a television in every room of the house.

When I was a child, it was a huge, huge luxury to have one television set. We had one little black and white TV set with a screen the size of a handkerchief. Now we have television sets with screens the size of the state of Montana. And we have one in every room of the house—or at least one on every floor. One upstairs in the bedroom, one downstairs in the recreation room, one in the living room, perhaps a smaller one in the kitchen.

And we don't know how to survive without our "stuff." If the cable goes out, and we can't get television, we're dead! We don't know even how to talk to each other anymore.

You know, like . . . let's just get some cheese and crackers out, with some apple juice or some wine, and sit in the living room and talk to each other. *It would be incomprehensible.* "You mean we're going spend from six o'clock in the evening until ten o'clock, when we go to bed, *talking?* Are you kidding me?"

Or, God forbid, *reading a good book?*

So the answer to your question is that people return to their life-styles *because they don't know any other way to live.* They have not been shown or trained in any other way to live.

But we don't have to give up our possessions in order to claim our identity. It's perfectly okay to have a television in every room of the house, you know, and three cars in the driveway, and whatever else it pleases you to enjoy, in terms of your physical accouterment. It's perfectly fine to do that. There's nothing inherently wrong with that, and it won't damage you in any way or curtail your spiritual growth, as long as it hasn't overtaken your ability to identify with Who You Really Are, and to demonstrate and express that in your experience.

To the degree that your possessions stop you from expressing and experiencing Who You Really Are, then to that degree your possessions have gotten the best of you. That is, they have *literally* gotten the *best* of you! But to the degree that you're using your possessions to facilitate the demonstration and experience of Who You Really Are, then those possessions actually wind up being tools that you use beneficially to generate larger and larger expressions of your true identity.

So the possessions themselves are not the issue.

DR. COOPER: Do you mean if our possessions serve a spiritual purpose, they are okay, but if we are mistakenly allowing them to tie us to our "story" (or to what we "have"), then they are not serving us?

I'm not quite sure I'm following everything here.

I get that our "possessions" are not Who We Are, but I have also been taught—as has been the Cultural Message for as long as most of us can remember—that "becoming established" and "getting our act together" (when it comes to what we "have") is key to a successful life and to a life well-lived.

How does what you are saying tie into what the Cultural Story tells us about our possessions?

NEALE: I don't disagree with you that that has been the Cultural Message. And by the way, some of the possessions that I have in my own life, just to use myself as an example, have no apparent spiritual value or benefit—no way to bring benefit to the process of expressing my true self . . . unless I include as my identity that I am a being, an essence in the universe, who enjoys "enjoying Self." *There's a place in life for us to enjoy ourselves.*

So I don't apologize for the fact that I have a television set in my living room with a screen as big as the state of Montana, because I enjoy watching a good movie, and I enjoy watching sports events. And that's okay with me. I had to really allow myself to bring that device into my living room, my big screen television set, and be okay with the fact that I derive enjoyment, recreation, from it.

Because to the degree that I allow myself enjoyment, to the degree that I allow myself to have a good time—to have wonderful recreation— to that degree I can re-create myself anew in the next grandest version of the greatest vision ever I held about Who I Am.

It's clear to me that the happier I am, the happier that I can make other people around me. So I'm in favor of material possessions that bring happiness to me. And I'm very grateful that my life has provided me with the wherewithal to provide myself with those kinds of physical possessions.

So the possessions don't have to serve what looks to some people like a "spiritual purpose." Being happy *is* a spiritual purpose. Yet if I provided myself with those possessions in a way that stopped me from sharing my happiness with anybody else, then I would consider that I had been overtaken by my possessions. So I make certain that, financially and in other ways, I share abundantly with all those whose lives I touch. This allows me then to feel very good about sharing with myself as well.

I put myself on the list of people I love enough to go out and obtain the possessions that I have, to make myself feel happy and at peace and good about the life that I'm living. I'm not suggesting for one minute that my possessions are the *source* of my feeling happy and at peace. But they certainly assist me in having a joyful experience of life, and allow me to continue to experience myself as one who is happy, and can therefore share happiness and, for that matter, actually *provide happiness* for others.

DR. COOPER: Absolutely! I love the statement you have made at several of your retreats: *"Include yourself in the circle of people you love."*

Let's move on now to the next questions: *Where am I?* and *Why am I where I am?*

In many of your presentations, you invite the audience members to make an important decision. You ask them to consider whether they see themselves as *Chemical Creatures*—that is, nothing more than "logical biological incidents" that happened to emerge from mother and father—or whether they, in fact, see themselves as *Spiritual Beings*.

People attending your presentations and reading the *Conversations with God* material have presumably made the latter decision—that we are Spiritual Beings choosing to have a Human Experience. *And this is not an insignificant "remembrance."* In fact, it is a remembrance that changes everything!

If we are, in fact, Spiritual Beings having a Human Experience, we can infer that we have *chosen* to come to Earth for a very specific reason—one that beautifully and gloriously serves the Agenda of our Soul. That is, no matter how much of a "struggle" it may *appear* to be here, physical life is, in fact, a *gift,* when we can remember our true identity and use it to navigate our day-to-day encounters in an entirely different way.

Like the people of Ouagadougou, who found happiness even in the most trying of times, when we have a willingness to explore *where we are* and *why we are where we are,* we open the gateway to finding happiness and fulfillment, no matter what is going around us. We understand that we have *chosen* to be here for a specific reason that *serves us* (and that serves the Agenda of our Soul), and we can then begin to see past struggle and to "see the gift," *as we reconsider what any given day or any given moment is about.*

NEALE: Struggle disappears when one answers those questions with clarity, and with the wisdom of the soul . . . providing the response, *"There is no such thing as struggle."*

Not only does struggle cease in any given moment, it literally dissolves and it disappears from our life. It ceases to have its illusory form. *All struggle disappears.* There is no such thing as struggle when an entity, a sentient being, has answered for themselves who they are and why they are here.

In fact, struggle turns into *celebration.*

All struggle becomes celebration, ultimately, in the mind of the Master, who understands that every circumstance and condition has been produced co-jointly, by all of the souls collaboratively creating that experience or that event, in order that each of the souls might have a perfect contextual field within which to announce and to declare, to express and to fulfill at the next level, Who They Really Are.

This is about spiritual growth. This is about spiritual expansion. This is about the soul's evolution.

And so Spiritual Masters celebrate *every* circumstance and condition, though this may be difficult for the normal human mind to comprehend.

And in the celebration of the circumstance and the condition that some may call "negative," *the circumstance and the condition itself begins to transform.* This is because the vibratory frequency of celebratory energy, which is so powerful and positive, has a positive effect on the exterior physical expressions of life.

And *gratitude*, by the way, is the foundational energy of all celebration. When we are *grateful* for the situation previously thought of as stressful, that gratitude turns stress into celebration and can produce remarkably different results and outcomes, both internally in the way we are experiencing life, as well as externally in the way that life itself is expressing.

That is, when we hold the experience that we're now moving through differently inside of ourselves (as a celebration of our true identity, providing an opportunity to demonstrate it, rather than an obstacle to that demonstration), the resulting shift in the energy we are feeling and projecting begins to produce outcomes outside of ourselves that can sometimes be remarkably altered, from a purely physical point of view.

Ancient alchemists called those altered outcomes *miracles*, and that's how miracles are produced. *It's the alchemy of the universe.*

When we understand that Who We Are is pure energy, the Essential Essence of Life itself, and that this energy not only composes us and comprises us, but is projected through us, from us, and outward into the world . . . and when we understand furthermore that energy affects other energy, that all energy *impacts* other energy . . . then we begin to understand that how we *think* about a thing determines how the thing is, and continues to be. Or, as physicists have put it: "Nothing that is observed is unaffected by the observer." This is pure physics. This is pure *science*.

When we understand this, stressful situations can be transformed in a remarkable way, because we don't hold them anymore as stressful situations, but rather, as opportunities for, and platforms upon which we can enjoy, the celebration, the wonder, and the glory of Who We Really Are.

DR. COOPER: What a point of view to hold! And it seems to me that the key ingredient in that process of gratitude and celebration *is the willingness to open your mind to go there.*

In medicine alone, I have witnessed times when a patient has come in with an "illness" that has a certain "expected outcome," which may be perceived as negative. Perhaps they are told that they have only a couple of years, or a couple of months for that matter, to live. And if a doctor gives a patient a prognosis like that, and the patient becomes resigned to it being true, then it likely will be.

Yet there are countless stories of "medical miracles"—things that are unexplainable by modern medicine—that are so often linked to those people who had the willingness to go to the place of *acceptance, gratitude, and yes, even celebration,* despite what appeared to be occurring in their lives and the seemingly tragic nature of it.

The courageous young woman Amy Purdy, who was recently featured on Oprah's Super Soul Sunday and released a book called *On My Own Two Feet,* is a powerful example of this.[1] She was a professional snowboarder aiming for the Olympics who, at the young age of nineteen, became severely ill with bacterial meningitis. She was hospitalized with "less than a 2 percent chance to live."

She was brought into the operating room, knowing she would be having both of her legs amputated, in addition to having her spleen and kidneys removed. She did survive the operation but, needless to say, her quality of life was drastically altered and only a fraction of what it was prior to her illness.

However, as she was learning to live with her handicap, Amy Purdy asked herself the following life-altering question: *"If my life were a book and I were the author, how would I want the story to end?"*

And from that moment on Amy began to visualize a new life.

Although she could not snowboard like she used to, she would imagine every day getting back on the slopes and how it would feel to have that experience again. She never once let go of her vision of Who She Dreamed To Be, even in the face of overwhelming adversity.

That simple yet profound question, *"If my life were a book and I were the author, how would I want the story to end?"*, ignited Amy's passion to make the most of her life. It was by no means an easy road, but she did, in fact, regain her ability to snowboard, ultimately earning herself the bronze medal at the Paralympics.

But even more inspiring—*even more inspiring than that*—was the *inner transformation* that took place along the way. For Amy realized that *who you show up as* in the face of challenge is what defines who you are. It relates back to our willingness to answer the question for ourselves of *why we are here* on the planet to begin with.

Amy Purdy has become a global spokesperson and a mentor helping others with disabilities, spreading her message to the world at large about what it means to never give up on living what she calls *an inspired life.* And Amy is just one example.

I can't tell you how many patients I have met who have transformed "devastating diagnoses" into stepping stones toward spiritual enlightenment. *Talk about "seeing the gift" in even the worst of times.*

And every time I hear about, or witness, a story like that, it gives me chills—because it is exactly what we've been talking about, *demonstrated with clarity in these people's lives.*

And it does, in turn, affect their outcome.

There is no doubt in my mind about that.

These are the people—if anyone is going to recover "miraculously," or turn their life into something profoundly meaningful following a devastating illness, as Amy did—*this is the energetic framework from which it occurs*, in my observation.

NEALE: You're correct, in my experience as well, that *acceptance of "what is"* and seeing it as a gift allowing us to experience and demonstrate who we are, is the most powerful response that a person could possibly give to circumstances, events, and situations that could be defined by a person who's not spiritually aware as stressful. And so stress turns into celebration when we move to step one, the first of the three steps that you articulated a minute ago: *acceptance of exactly what is so.*

What's So is *What's So*, and that's what's true about that.

And as *Conversations with God* says: "What you resist persists, and what you look at disappears. That is, it ceases to have its illusory form."

Or, as spiritual teacher Da Free John put it, eloquently I thought, in his prescription to turn stress into celebration: "Cease all Againstness."

DR. COOPER: Yes, I like that.

NEALE: When I first heard that, I thought, "What a remarkable formula, in three words."

Cease all Againstness.

Therein lies the wonder and the glory of Who You Are. Because when you cease to be against what's going on, you embrace and accept what is happening, and transform it, however it turns out—whether, in fact, you do leave your physical body in three or four months, or you live for another five or ten years. Either way, it's totally okay, because you're not against what is occurring.

As my friend Byron Katie puts it: "Stop arguing with life."

DR. COOPER: Ha-ha! Yeah! Well, it seems to me like you're ceasing to hold onto your illusory story, which is not Who You Are. And I think it's the holding onto the "story" which produces the resistance; in other words, it is the expectation that things be a certain way, and if they're not, then not being okay with that.

But I think the moment we cease holding onto our "story" . . .

NEALE: . . . our struggles disappear.

DR. COOPER: Exactly! And as you said at your last retreat, which I love: "Ground zero is the best place to be." Because ground zero is the *basis of all creation.*

You are then invited to look at your life from a whole new perspective, which is not one contained within the bounds of your previous "story" of how it should be, but rather like an empty canvas with all of your paints waiting for you to paint whatever picture you want. That is, whatever response to the circumstances that would best serve the *Agenda of your Soul.*

And all of this brings us to the fourth question. Given that I've decided who I am, where I am, and why I'm here, *what do I intend to do about that?*

You can then take any circumstance and, from "ground zero," from the fundamental platform of creativity, you get full choice as to how to respond in that moment as the highest demonstration of Who You Are.

NEALE: Yes. That's the moment of definition. As *Conversations with God* says: "Every act is an act of self-definition."

And in the moment when we answer "What do I intend to do about that?", we are really saying, "This is how I currently define myself. This is how I define Who I Really Am. This is how I define Divinity, as a matter of fact."

One day I'm going to write a book called *Demonstrating Divinity*, and in it I'm going to offer the idea that defining Divinity is the process by which we say, "this is what God is" in this particular circumstance, in this situation. *I know you know what God is, and what Divinity is, but I'm now going to show you, in case you might have forgotten.*

And that's really what all Great Masters have done. Whether we're talking about Lao Tzu or Buddha, whether we're talking about Moses or Jesus, Mother Mary or Mother Theresa, Mohammed or any of the Great Masters, male or female, ancient or contemporary, they all moved through the world in such a way that their demonstration of Divinity defined Divinity. We now *call* that Divine, because of their demonstration.

DR. COOPER: So we are here to define the Divine. *Conversations with God* also says that our life lived is our most powerful message to the world . . .

NEALE: And to ourselves.

DR. COOPER: Yes!

NEALE: We're not even here to send a message to the world.

That happens automatically.

We're here simply to send a message *to ourselves*—that is, to remind ourselves—so that we might fully remember, and then fully express, Who We Really Are, thus to complete in that moment the Agenda of the Soul, over and over again, moving through all the moments, days, and years of our life, coming to *Completion* in the process of remembering Who We Really Are through the demonstration and the expression of it. Not so that the world is in some way impacted, *but because our own personal agenda invites us to do so.*

However, when we do this, the world is inevitably touched by it, because this sort of demonstration is remarkably impacting upon the physical environment, for the simple reason that—as I have noted now a number of times—energy impacts upon energy itself.

So it has been said that if a Christ, for instance, were to walk down the middle of a battlefield between two opposing armies, the members of those armies would lay down their arms. They would lay down their arms simply because of his presence there. And that's what happens when Who We Are is expressed fully in us, through us, *as* us, as part of our own evolutionary process, without seeking directly to affect or change the world. It simply does so automatically, because of the impact that Energy has on Energy Itself.

We are talking about The Essential Essence interacting with the Essential Essence.

By the way, doctors know all about this. What I've just said is something that everyone in the medical profession either knows . . . or should know. That the very way they walk into a room . . . you know, a doctor needs to understand that as soon as she puts on her white coat, and as soon as he puts the stethoscope around his neck, they might as well put a badge on that says: "I am a Healer. I am a Doctor. And you're going to be okay." Or, at least you're going to be as okay as the physical experiences that you're now moving through will allow you to be. And *metaphysically,* you can be totally, *totally* okay.

Most physicians don't understand that they are also metaphysicians. That is, they are larger than physicians. They are *meta*-physicians. But only one out of a hundred doctors understands this. Those who do understand are said to have developed an extraordinary "bedside manner," *because they understand who they are when they walk into the room of a patient.* That they're not just Physicians, they're Metaphysicians. That is, *they're larger than that.* Even as Life is not simply physical, it is metaphysical. It's larger than simply the physical.

So when doctors understand that—when more people in the medical profession understand that energy impacts upon energy itself—they will walk into every room in an entirely different way. *No matter how busy they are.*

DR. COOPER: Absolutely! And I think that often, in the rush of things at the hospital, it can be viewed as the "nice doctors" who are willing to offer that extra dose of compassion and understanding. People sometimes don't "get" why certain doctors might take more time to do that; however, for me, having been exposed to your work, I see clearly that the reason isn't just about offering more compassion or understanding to the patient. I believe *we give at least as much to ourselves* in being willing to "show up" in that sort of a way.

For me, beginning to walk into the room in that way was the beginning of remembering Who I Really Am, and realizing that *I loved how it felt to show up like that.* So it's about re-uniting with your own soul … with the piece of you that, deep down, you desire to express and to bring forth in that moment.

As you said just a moment ago, I think it is about daring to show up *in a way that is Divine.*

NEALE: Everybody is a minister, everybody is a doctor, and everybody in the world is a healer.

All we're doing on the planet is helping each other.

All of the professions, all of the occupations—I don't care if you're a butcher, a baker, or a candlestick maker, you know . . . I don't care if you're a florist, or a gas station attendant, or a plumber, or a lawyer, or a doctor—all that anyone is doing is helping someone else. We're all helping each other. That's what we're doing.

So, in whatever occupation you have, do you see yourself as helping another? And if you see yourself as doing so, as a means of expressing an aspect of yourself—*as a demonstration of Who You Really Are*—suddenly your whole relationship to your occupation will change dramatically. And so, too, will the way that the people you serve *receive* what it is that you are offering.

So whether you're a doctor walking into a patient's room, or a gas station attendant walking up to a car, it doesn't really matter. The process is the same and the effect is the same: helping and healing.

Elisabeth Kübler-Ross, who I had the great joy of working with for a period of time in my life as one of her staff assistants, used to say this. She would respond to people who asked her how she was able to be such a wonderful presence in the life of her patients such that she would walk into the room and people would immediately feel better, just because of her presence.

She once made this comment, in front of a large room full of medical students: "Oh, I see. You think it's because I'm a doctor. But I want to tell you," she went on in her Swiss accent, "that the lady who comes in behind me to clean the toilet and mop up the floor has an equal effect on the patients. And I can't tell you how many patients have gotten better because of the lady who's cleaning the bathroom. So if you think it's my occupation that creates that effect, you do not understand what's happening here."

So it is important to see that we are *all* in the helping professions. *There's nobody who's not.*

Everything we do helps someone else.

And to that degree we are rewarded internally and, as well, often, externally. That is, people give *us* stuff (money, etc.) for the help we've given *them*. Everybody on the planet is in the helping profession, and everybody can feel like a doctor or a minister walking into a room. Everyone can feel that sense of self-fulfillment and full expression of the most wondrous part of themselves, whether they're a doctor or a minister or a person with flowers at the flower store, or candy at the sweetshop, or magazines and papers at the news stand, or legal advice in a lawyer's office—or a mommy or daddy at home, offering humankind the greatest gift it could ever receive: the love and nurturing of its offspring.

It doesn't really matter what you do, only how you are helping and what you are *being* while you are doing it.

DR. COOPER: I love how you transform "work," which I perhaps previously would have considered an "obligation," a "social responsibility," or a "less than fun thing to do," and make it into what seems like a very *exciting* and "soul-serving" thing to do.

You make me very *excited* to wake up and to serve in that kind of a way!

NEALE: It's the most exciting thing that anybody could do!

It's what gets me jumping out of bed in the morning! Exactly, at 71 going on 72, hopping out of bed nevertheless with the same amount of excitement that I had when I was 21 and imagined that I was doing it for a different reason.

But now at 71 going on 72, I jump out of bed at five o'clock in the morning, unable to wait to get started with the day, with another chance to self-express and to demonstrate to myself the highest notion I ever had about Who I Really Am. And to do so in such a way that I wind up *loving myself, loving life, and loving all the conditions of life that have allowed me to do that.*

If that doesn't make one fall in love with God, then nothing will.

Chapter Two

DISSECTING THE TRUTH:
A Look at the Human Body

DR. COOPER: That was beautiful.

NEALE: Life is beautiful. It's just a matter of seeing it that way.

DR. COOPER: Yes, I get that. I really do. And I really *want* to embrace this optimistic viewpoint you have. It all seems so magnificent, so wonderful, so freeing!

And I do agree—*that the point of life is what we make it.* That we have the immense *privilege* to select in every golden moment of Now who we next choose to be, and how we next choose to "show up."

But I do have a few more questions for you.

NEALE: Yes . . . How may I serve you?

DR. COOPER: Well, it's all very nice to understand *conceptually* that we are Spiritual Beings, here to fulfill the Agenda of the Soul. And to understand that all struggle can turn to celebration when we dare to ask ourselves, and to *create the answers to,* the Seven Simple Questions and the Four Fundamental Questions of Life.

And I really "get" that this is possible.

I mean, your stories from the people of Ouagadougou are living proof that it's possible to live in this sort of a way—with peace, harmony, joy, and unity among people, despite being among what we would clearly call "the disadvantaged people of this world."

I mean, it is *remarkable*—living with one light bulb that has to be traded with the rare appliances they may use during the daytime when light is not needed. Living in dried mud huts or concrete dwellings, with no such things as professional careers or financial success or exotic vacations as we have it here in North America. *And still these people arguably have more love and happiness in their hearts than could be bought with all of the wealth on the planet!*

So clearly it illustrates that there is "something more" going on here—another reason for being on the planet—and that it is this "spiritual journey" we have come here to continue. A spiritual journey that has much more to do with how we are *being* than what we are *doing.*

But Neale, as I sit here listening, I still feel somewhat shocked at how this is all possible . . .

Because even as you're telling me that it's true that we can live this way—and you have visited 26 nations on the planet, some of which have clearly *demonstrated* this way of living—I still find myself not quite sure how to apply this wisdom in my everyday 9-to-5 life here in the Western World. As you said yourself, *it goes against all we have been taught and trained to do.* So many of us do not understand how to "survive" within this new way of holding life. Even myself, who has been practically "raised by Neale Donald Walsch," find myself struggling with it at times!

NEALE: And why are you struggling with it? Why aren't you celebrating it?

DR. COOPER: Because at times it feels like I have to make a choice. A choice between serving the Agenda of Physical Life—everything from the perceived "needs of my family," to my job and income, to how I'm going to pay the next rent bill and get food on the table—and serving the Agenda of my Soul. And I'm not quite sure how the two can co-exist in a way where one complements the other.

So I think some clarification would be helpful here. Because I've noticed that people, myself included, often experience spirituality and physicality as if they were two separate aspects of life, rather than seeing them as linked at the most fundamental level (which, of course, they are).

But it is nevertheless hard to truly *live that way.*

NEALE: I think we have a very powerful point to make here—this business of the *Intersection between physicality and spirituality* that not so many people really experience. They may think of them together *conceptually,* but in terms of their actual *on-the-ground experience* they may hold them entirely differently, thinking that one's physical expressions and experiences are *other* than, or *different* from, one's spiritual expressions and experiences.

And maybe the purpose of this whole dialogue that we're having might be to impress upon people not only the significance of the fact that there is no separation between our physical and spiritual experience, but that the co-mingling of the two is exactly what life was intended to produce, it is our *reason for existing*—and that when we understand this, our *whole lives will change.*

DR. COOPER: Yes! It is an important concept to touch on. And it's absolutely been my observation that, even among people who would consider themselves to be "very spiritual"—I've been to a number of your retreats, and a lot of the people there would consider themselves to have spirituality as an integral component of their lives—I've still observed, as I mentioned before, people going home and returning to their lives *and still living as if there is separation between the physical and the spiritual.*

Perhaps they wake up in the morning and meditate for a while, which appears to be a spiritual aspect of life, and then they go to work, and that appears to be a physical aspect of life.

I've observed this in friends I have met at your retreats, as well as in spiritual coaching clients who have come to me for the very reason that they want help implementing spirituality in an ongoing way in their lives. And I think it's a struggle for much of humanity to really understand how to live our moment-to-moment existence as not only a physical entity, but also a spiritual entity—*and to have a moment-to-moment spiritual experience as well.* That is, to understand how to really put these spiritual concepts *on the ground* in day-to-day life.

There is a story I would like to insert and share here, Neale . . . one that I think is fitting to what we're talking about.

NEALE: Go ahead.

DR. COOPER: I would like to describe the moment I first realized we are "more than our bodies" . . . because I remember this vividly.

It was the moment I entered the anatomy lab in my first year of medical school. However, this was no ordinary anatomy lab. It was one where we actually *dissected human cadavers* over the course of two years.

We dissected everything from the heart to the lungs to the muscles and nerves, and even to the brain and spinal cord. We delved into the deepest understandings that science and neuroscience can provide about who we are, *actually being able to see and visualize it right before our eyes.* It was one of the most striking things I ever witnessed in my life. And certainly not an experience that many people come across at the age of twenty.

I can tell you that prior to this experience I was very attached to my physical body being Who I Am. However, the time I spent in that lab dramatically changed my understanding.

What struck me most was *the total lifelessness of the bodies before me.* As they were lying on the lab benches and we went to make the first cut with the scalpel, all I knew *without a shadow of a doubt was that this is not the human being. This is not the person!*

And it became absolutely clear to me that the mere "physical body" had very little to do with the person who had walked on this Earth.

Although people may understand this *conceptually*, to actually see it and experience it is both startling and eye-opening, to say the least. And the thing is, it wasn't just a hunch. It wasn't just a subtle feeling that there was "something more going on." It was an *undeniable truth*, and I believe that anyone standing in my shoes would have seen, and *known*, the exact same thing: that without that "added presence"—that spiritual quality, if you could call it such—our bodies have little to do with who we are.

It then poses the question, *"Who are we really?"*

And it invites us to consider: how, if at all, does this "extra presence" play a role in the day-to-day, moment-to-moment unfolding of our lives?

NEALE: It sure does pose the question. Thank you.

DR. COOPER: You know, Neale, when I was in that lab as a young student, my mind went to the place of: "My gosh, what if this were my parent whose cadaver was lying here?" And that thought scared me! It scared me that the sum total of someone I loved could disappear at the moment their body "crossed over."

This is why the revelation that we are more than our bodies brought me such comfort. Because I could see the truth right before my eyes that even if that was my mother's body lying there, *I would know that it was not her.*

Many people have asked me, "How did you know that?"

It's not an easy thing to explain, but what I tell them is that the skin on the cadaver was hardened and rubbery and so pale; the body was utterly limp. The face was expressionless to the point of being almost unrecognizable—no smile, eyes closed, and none of the expressions that previously shone on the face of that person.

I think that when we *mistake* our loved one's *body* for Who They Are, it is because we are seeing the *energy* that *animates* physical form— the joy sparkling in their eyes, the dance of a smile on their lips, or even the tears of sadness falling upon their cheek. We're seeing the human emotions and characteristics, both the good and the bad, that shape the *expression* of that body, and give us the *experience* of Who They Are. We're seeing invisible energy made visible, metaphysical life made physical.

But anyone who would have seen the utter lifelessness of these cadavers would have known—and would have literally *seen*—that when this "presence," the energy, was gone, the disintegrating remains had very little, or perhaps nothing at all, to do with the person who once inhabited that body.

NEALE: What a surreal experience.

DR. COOPER: Yes! I wish you could have been there to see it, Neale. In fact, I think it's an experience that would profoundly change almost anyone's life.

Here I was, sitting in that lab day after day, with the professors describing the intricate workings of the human body from birth to death and every moment in-between. Yet something about the purely medical and scientific theory just didn't sit right with me. *Intuitively, I felt like it was an incomplete way of looking at life.*

The feeling that "there must be more" was most noticeable in the neuroanatomy portion of the lab, where we spent two months dissecting the brain and spinal cord. I was literally *holding a brain in my hands*, tracing the pathways with my scalpel, and being told: "These are the pathways of people's emotions. This is what creates who we are. This is our personality," and so on.

Yet all I could think to myself was, "No, this is not who we are! I don't believe you. This can't be who we are!" *It just didn't make sense.*

In my experience, and from what I felt in my heart and soul, this could not be who we are. But the professors were telling me, "This is who we are." It was a very odd, and somewhat disconcerting, experience . . .

And it certainly caused me to have a second thought—to do a double take—on what was really going on here.

NEALE: Interesting. *How interesting.*

How does the body remain pliable enough to dissect it? I mean, wouldn't it just get, like, rigor mortis?

DR. COOPER: They do preserve it in some way that makes it easy to dissect, although I'm not sure the exact chemicals they use, or how they specifically go about the embalming process.

I do know, from experience, that they drain the blood out of the body and replace it with something that hardens, like plastic, so it is much easier to dissect that way.

NEALE: I'm almost sorry I asked that! How did you remove such memories from your mind, and allow your mind to get back to, you know, seeing people in their real form, without imagining all of those memories?

I mean, I'm too sensitive; I wouldn't be able to deal with that for five minutes.

DR. COOPER: Well, the professor did ask me in the first session, "Are you going to pass out? Do you need to sit down?" It is quite a shock to be exposed to this sort of thing!

And it's true that I would go through my life after a lab session— say we just looked at the lungs—and I would be thinking so much about people's lungs. I guess that's a weird way to walk through the world, but I'd be thinking and imagining people's lungs as I was talking to them, because it was such a strong memory in my mind.

But overall, I really just didn't *believe* what they were teaching me in that lab—in the spiritual sense—so I don't think I took it too seriously. To me, it simply illustrated that I was connecting with my family, my loved ones, and every single person whose path I crossed, at the level of *energy.* It confirmed the existence of *something beyond the physical.*

To me, it made that crystal clear.

NEALE: *The body is not by any means the sum total of Who We Are.* You are very lucky to have gained that insight at such a young age.

There are a great many people who don't ever get that "knowing," that deep understanding, in their entire lifetime on the planet.

DR. COOPER: This was the first occurrence in my life that really placed the question in front of me: *If we are not our bodies, then who are we?*

It was, in effect, the beginning of an exploration of exactly what we talked about earlier—*the intersection of physicality and spirituality*—and understanding the link between the body and the soul.

And Neale, I would like to share one more story that adds to this one, which made my understanding even deeper. It was the first open-heart surgery that I attended—a coronary artery bypass surgery—which is when someone needs the arteries fixed around their heart.

What caught my attention with this surgery is that it's an operation on the *heart*—one of the most vital organs in the body. It's not like the patient has just broken a leg or something, and we have to fix it. The heart is one of the things that we would view as most crucial to keeping us alive. I mean, *without a beating heart, who are we?*

So I was intrigued about this surgery from the moment I walked into the room.

I vividly remember standing in the operating room and helping out the anesthetist, who was putting the patient "to sleep" for the operation. And one thing that struck me in this moment is that, in order to put a patient "to sleep"—most people don't know this, but we have to paralyze their muscles. Because if we're going to put a breathing tube in, and their muscles are not paralyzed, they will reject the breathing tube. That is, they won't relax enough to let it in. We also don't want the patient to reject the surgery, or to "fight back" (as their muscular reflexes will counteract what the surgeon is trying to do), so this is another reason that temporary paralysis is needed before making the first incision.

We then bring the patient's state of consciousness all the way down to what one might call a "drug-induced coma." What this means is that when the patient is undergoing surgery, they are not actually in the state of "sleep," where one might have dreams or other relatively active patterns of brain activity. Rather, if we were to measure the patient's brain activity on an EEG (an electroencephalogram), it would show a pattern equivalent to being completely unconscious and comatose.[2]

Also, when the patient "wakes up" from the surgery, assuming that the anesthetic was administered correctly, they will have total amnesia around it; that is, they will have *no recollection that the surgery ever took place,* save the remnant wounds of the operation.

If this all sounds kind of like "science fiction," don't feel alone. This is exactly how I felt when I was present in the room, observing, as a young medical student. But it is real. And it is *remarkable.*

Getting back to this patient, he also could not breathe for himself (since his muscles were paralyzed), so we had to "breathe" for him using ventilation techniques. And furthermore, because this particular surgery involved the heart, his heart was no longer beating while we worked on it. Instead, he was attached to a "cardiopulmonary bypass machine"—tubing that carried his blood and circulated it around and oxygenated it, performing the functions that the heart and lungs normally do.[3]

So here I was, standing in the operating room, with the patient's blood being pumped in tubes that stretched around the room—no beating heart, no functional lungs, no active memory, his brain activity depressed to the level of someone who is comatose, and his muscles paralyzed. I remember thinking to myself in that moment, "Oh, my gosh, if this doesn't cause us to question Who We Are?"; if this doesn't cause us to take a double take on "What is life?", then what would?

Take away our heart, our brain function, our lungs, our muscles, and *Who Are We?*

So the biggest thing I learned from these experiences in medical school is that physicality and spirituality are not separate. Our physical selves, clearly, to me, are *nothing* without that constant and eternal link to the spiritual energy, and this became evidently clear to me in those moments.

NEALE: So what you're saying is that there is an *energetic component to life* that animates all of physicality. An Essential Essence.

And, thinking through what I've just heard you say, obviously what they're doing in the operating room is . . . they're applying substitutes for the mechanisms of the body. And they have a substitute for the heart, which substitutes for the heart's mechanism, a substitute for the lungs, and so forth. But the Essential Essence must be remaining with that body—otherwise it would be a cadaver. Because *there is no substitute for the fundamental energy of life when that energy of life is no longer flowing to the body,* and that fundamental energy is *not flowing from any machine.*

DR. COOPER: That's a good way of looking at it!

NEALE: So how does this relate to a person who is not under sedation, and walking around living a normal life?

DR. COOPER: Well, to me, how I took that and applied it to my own everyday life—obviously not under sedation—is I thought to myself: *It is clear, without a doubt, that there is this spiritual energy that animates our physical presence, which can't be substituted for.*

It is also clear that we don't see it as such, generally. Most of humankind does not see this remarkable tool that we have!

Conversations with God talks about the eternal link we have to God, and with this comes the idea that spirituality can help us in times of challenge or hardship or struggle. And yet ironically, when we find ourselves in times of challenge, hardship, or struggle, I have observed that much of humankind will resort to "physical" solutions to the problem and not even consider a spiritual point of view.

For me, *when I started to see before my very own eyes that this spiritual presence always accompanies us*, it made it less of an esoteric concept and more of a real down-to-Earth thing. I began to embrace the idea that not only is this "spiritual presence" with me in every moment of every day, *it actually is Who I Am*.

And if it is Who I Am, then *it must be able to be used as a wonderfully assistive tool in my toolbox of how to walk through my life.*

NEALE: So if this Spiritual Energy is Who We Are—if that is what you're telling me—then how come it automatically leaves the body if the heart stops functioning?

What is the reason—what is the connection—when the heart stops functioning? If there is no substitute mechanism, no machine in an operating room keeping things going . . . you're on the street hit by a car and you can't get to the hospital fast enough, and there is no substitute functioning for the heart—the heart just stops beating—it's over. Then this "presence" you are talking about, this life force, leaves you, presumably. So the spiritual aspect of Who You Are *appears to be dependent on the physical mechanism of the body in order to remain with the body.*

And when the physical mechanism fails—that is, when the heart stops beating—then the spiritual essence apparently has no choice but to say: "Well, take care of yourself, we're out of here. Bye-bye!" *And the Spiritual Essence leaves.*

So the question becomes, "What comes first, the chicken or the egg?"

Does the spiritual essence make a decision to leave, at some level of spiritual functioning, and is that what *causes* the heart to stop beating if it doesn't have a substitute mechanism? Or, does the heart stop beating *first*, and *then* the spiritual mechanism says: "Well, if you're not going to keep beating, I'm out of here!"

And what comes first, the chicken or the egg?

And the question is posed in reverse, or course, at birth. In the first moments of life. And by the way, this is a question that doctors have been debating and society has been debating for several thousand years: *When does physical life begin?*

Does life as we have defined it begin at the first beat of the heart in utero; when the fetus is in the mother's womb and it's just an inert mass of cells, until the first heartbeat and then suddenly, one presumes, we say it's alive!? Or, do we say it's not alive until it's actually been given birth, until it actually exits the mother's body?

So the *Intersection between physicality and spirituality* seems to me to be where it's at. And we have to pose the question: where do the physical and the spiritual energy intersect . . . and in a sense collide.

I once wrote a little booklet called *Heart Start, Love Start* with a maternity ward nurse who wanted to address the question, *When does life begin?* At the moment of birth, or at the moment that the heart starts in utero? Or, even before then?

Medical science now says it's when the embryo becomes "viable." And "viable" is understood to mean that the embryo is able to live by itself outside the womb.

But, spiritually speaking, one could, and many have, argued that this is not true; that life does not start when the embryo becomes viable and is able to live outside the womb. Life begins when a body exists *inside* the womb, *at the moment the heart has started beating.*

"Oh, oh," the doctor says. "Oh, oh, I hear a heartbeat!" You know, the baby's heart has started beating. And somewhere between four and six weeks of gestation, one suspects, the heart starts beating. And I have been intrigued for fifty years by the question: *Why does the heart suddenly start beating? Who turned the switch? And, for that matter, who turns the switch off?*

DR. COOPER: Yeah, it's a fascinating question, the age-old question of *when does life begin*, as well as the question you asked before that: is spirituality in fact *dependent* on physicality for its expression in this world?

I want to divert for a minute here, Neale, and then get back to your question.

What I'd like to chat about for just a moment is genetics . . . branching into some new scientific discoveries around something called *epigenetics* (which is basically the *expression* of our genes . . . and we'll get to that in a minute).

Anyway, basically we have an entire genetic code, and every single cell in our body has the encoding for the *entire body* held within it. That is, the DNA of each cell is identical, and the only difference between different types of cells is which part of the genetic code is "active" (or "turned on") and which part is "inactive" (or "turned off").

The DNA (or genetic code) of a hair cell, to give an example, is the same as the DNA of a heart cell, a liver cell, *or any other cell in the body*. But each of these cells has "chosen" (early on in embryonic development) to express itself in a certain way, which results in the unique characteristics of each of them.

This process is called "stem cell differentiation"—which you explained very well at your last retreat.

NEALE: Thank you, doctor. I was trying to impress you. (Laughs.)

DR. COOPER: What I really want to focus on here is *epigenetics*— which is essentially the ability of any individual cell to modify its expression in subtle ways over the course of a person's life.

Cells no longer undergo *major* changes after the initial embryonic developmental stages are over—in other words, a heart cell is not suddenly going to become a liver cell—but they do continue to undergo *minor* changes all throughout our lives. In fact, our cells are continually modifying their genetic expression *every hour!*

So the genetic expression within any given cell at any given time is not "fixed," as many people think it is. *It is not a static thing.* Rather, it is continually adapting to both external and internal stimuli—*meaning that it adjusts to the environment and to any changes in the surroundings, as well as to any changes within the body itself.*

What's interesting about this is that there was a groundbreaking study released by Dr. Richard J. Davidson in 2013 in the *Journal of Psychoneuroendocrinology* talking about the "epigenetic effects of meditation" on the body—meaning that *actual changes can occur in our genes* as a result of mindfulness and meditation activities! [4]

When I read this study it immediately grabbed my attention, as I thought: *Here is real live proof that spirituality can impact our day-to-day on-the-ground physical lives!*

There was evidence right there on the page of this Intersection between physicality and spirituality that we have been talking about.

The study compared a control group of non-meditators to a group of experienced meditators who were instructed to engage in eight hours of "mindfulness activities" and, after only eight hours, there were already measurable genetic changes! These changes included reduced expression of inflammatory and pro-inflammatory genes, and reduced production of stress hormones such as cortisol as a result of altered genetic pathways.

The other interesting thing is that, prior to the eight-hour experiment, the genes of both the control group and the meditation group were evaluated *and found to be equivalent.* That is, the meditation group did not start out with an "advantage"; rather, the benefits of meditation *came from doing the activity itself.*

Anyway, it illustrates the profound link between our spiritual selves and our physical selves, for if our genetic expression can be changed in eight hours by a meditative/mindfulness experience, imagine the impact our "spiritual energy" can have on the body over an entire lifetime.

So returning to your question, Neale: if a person dies of their heart attack, is this just too bad for their soul, so to speak? Do they just have to move on and their body is "giving up on them"?

I don't think so. Extrapolating from studies such as this one, I would suggest that the body "giving up" is not done without the spiritual part interacting and contributing in some way to that process. It may not be done at a conscious level, but I think the soul is involved *at some level*, whether the person is consciously aware of it or not.

I think the body and the soul are intimately linked to one another, and that such incidents would occur *in concert with the agenda of both.*

NEALE: Interesting thought. And it reflects, absolutely, the information we were given in *HOME WITH GOD in a Life That Never Ends.* In that final book of the *CwG* nine-book dialogue series, we are told that no one dies at a time or in a way that is not of their choosing. Difficult as this is to believe at a purely physical, human level, we are invited in *CwG* to consider the possibility that nothing can happen to us—that is, to our body or mind—that is not done in accordance with the soul.

If we are truly Individuations of Divinity, this would have to be true, unless we concede that something can happen to God, or to any of God's Expressions, that is not Divine.

There are only two conclusions we can reach about Divinity and Humanity: that the two are intrinsically separate, or intrinsically united; that Divinity and Humanity are One Thing, or that Divinity and Humanity are two things—and that all of life, for that matter, is comprised of physical manifestations quite apart and separate from God.

Conversations with God tells us: "All things are One Thing. There is only One Thing, and all things are part of the One Thing there is."

It is that basis upon which all else that is contained in the 3,000+ pages of the *CwG* nine–book dialogue is based.

But let's get back to your discussion of stem cells. You appear to be suggesting, as a doctor, that stem cells differentiate at the behest of the Spirit. As you said, the mind—or the person's *state of being*, as you described in the meditation process—can have an influence on one's genetic and cellular expression.

So it seems to me the same thing could be happening in an embryo whose stem cells are in the process of differentiating. The *embryo's energy*, which could loosely be defined from a spiritual point of view to be its Essential Essence, may also be demonstrating its choices genetically and cellularly, and that this could happen *prior to the first heartbeat.* If those embryonic cells are moving and combining and forming and differentiating, then life *does,* in fact, happen prior to the first heartbeat. Because before the first heartbeat—in the first three to four to five weeks of the embryonic tissue's existence in the womb of the mother— bodily parts are being formed. Indeed, the heart *itself* is being formed! It doesn't beat before it's been formed.

Which means that there is decision-making activity at some level— that cells are differentiated by some process that begins before the heart starts beating.

Which invites an extraordinarily fascinating question: When does life actually *begin?*

Is Life Itself, in fact, part of the cellular activity of the sperm and the egg when they join together from the father and the mother, and is it, therefore, a fact that there's not an end or a beginning to life, but just a *transfer* of it? Could it be that life (the movement and decision-making of cells) simply transfers its intelligence from one life form to another? Is it possible that the tissue—the cellular mass—created by the mother's egg and the father's sperm joining together to form embryonic cellular existence, is not the *beginning* of "new" life, but simply a *continuation* of life, in yet another form, with no "break" in the line of energy of Essential Essence?

Is it possible that life doesn't really ever *begin,* but that it merely *continues?* And isn't it interesting to think in those terms that we are, as we're sitting here on this telephone talking, *the continuation of life from the very, very beginning of physical expression, thousands and thousands and thousands of years ago!?*

DR. COOPER: That is an incredible thought. I think you could be on to something here, Neale. I wouldn't be shocked if that's what science ends up proving a few years from now.

I think it's a remarkable thought.

NEALE: It requires life to be "pass-on-able"—but then, obviously, it *is* pass-on-able, because here we are, the descendants, if you please, of the very first human beings. Life, through the process of evolution, has created human beings, and we are the descendants of a never-ending transfer of Essential Essence, Divine Intelligence, that has always existed, and always will exist, in physicality.

But what about the cadaver?

Well, if life is defined as *motion*, and if you were to slice open a cadaver and examine it at the cellular level, even though the body is presumably dead you would still see *motion* at the sub-molecular level. This means that life never ends, but merely changes form.

Put under super ultra high microscopic examination, subject to the most powerful magnification, you would not see inert cells, their atoms and submolecular particles simply standing still. The energy that is animating the individual cells in the cadaver will still be moving. *That energy, that Essential Essence, not just frozen.*

Life *as we know it* may have ended, but *Life Itself* will have not.

DR. COOPER: I agree. And I think it would be even easier to understand if we imagined what would happen to a body in the natural world, rather than the artificial environment of a cadaver being dissected on a laboratory table in medical school.

If a human being passed away and the body was left in a forest or in the woods, and it disintegrated, then presumably its process of disintegration would fuel the growth of other things. As *Conversations with God* says, all life sustains life through the process of Life Itself.

So things that are so-called "dead organic material" are in fact growth factors, or substrates, for new life.

And if one were to look through a high-resolution electron micro-scope, one would indeed see *movement*, as you said—but this move-ment would serve a highly specific and valuable purpose, *which is to fuel the emergence of other life forms.*

NEALE: So it's not really a process of disintegration, it's a process of *inte-gration.*

DR. COOPER: Yes!

NEALE: The corpse that lies in the woods, in the forest, and ultimately "disintegrates" doesn't really "disintegrate" at all—it actually *inte-grates.* Or, if you please, *re-integrates, and becomes an integral part of the never-ending process and expression of life, simply in a different form.*

DR. COOPER: Exactly! I would agree. That is a beautiful way to put it—it feels so *complete. And wonderful, really.*

Like "death" is not so much of a death, but more of a never-ending cycle of existence furthering the propagation of life in a brand new way.

And perhaps our understanding that life never ends can facilitate a much fuller, richer life, because it has been said that our fear of death is directly proportional to our fear of life—of *living fully.*

NEALE: Yes, and I think our fear of death is really a fear of *losing our sense of Self,* of losing the present *form* in which our life is expressing.

In *HOME WITH God in a Life That Never Ends* I asked God, "What is death?", and God replied: "There's no such thing as death as you have imagined it. *What you call death is merely a process of re-identification.*"

So it turns out that life never, ever ends, but merely changes the form of its expression.

DR. COOPER: I like that idea.

NEALE: And the smallest part of you re-identifies in certain ways. In the analogy of the burning log in the fireplace, God asks, "Has the log disappeared, or has it merely changed the form in which it expresses, from wood, to flame, to heat, to smoke, and light?" The log has not disappeared, and the ashes in the fireplace are but the tiniest percentage, just as the cadaver is but the tiniest percentage, of the original physical expression. *The cadaver is analogous to the ashes of the log in the fireplace.* It is 0.05 percent of the life expression called a "human" that we can still see.

DR. COOPER: That's such a perfect comparison.

NEALE: Yes, it is for me.

Like the log's energy, which leaves its ashes behind—"ashes to ashes, dust to dust"—the human being leaves behind the tiniest percentage of what it was, and the grandest percentage goes on as other forms of energy. It simply expresses in different ways in the ultimate universe of physicality.

Interesting. *Interesting.*

We need to explore this further and see where it takes us.

Chapter Three

BEYOND THE BODY:
The Process of Creation

DR. COOPER: You know what I couldn't stop thinking about this past week, Neale?

NEALE: What's that?

DR. COOPER: The Intersection of physicality and spirituality. It's just so fascinating to think about.

I would like to start by saying that there was a very specific reason I brought up those medical examples last week—everything from dissecting the cadavers to the open heart surgery to the idea that we can "change our genes" with such simple things as changing our thoughts and our perceptions. I mean, they are remarkable stories, but on top of that there is a much more important reason I brought them up. And this is because, to me, they are a powerful illustration of this Intersection between physicality and spirituality that we are talking about here.

Conversations with God talks about the "three levels of awareness": *hope, faith, and knowing.* I would say that many people *hope* that they are more than their bodies—more than their physical existence here on the planet. And many people *hope* that the spiritual messages delivered by countless teachers across the globe can be true in their lives. *But many people do not necessarily experience this.* That is, they may say their "positive affirmations" and try to believe that things will work out in their favor, but the events and outcomes in their lives may not seem to confirm that this is true for them.

What I learned through my experiences in medicine—and perhaps most powerfully of all, in seeing the dead cadavers—was that I came to the *knowing* (not the *hoping*, but the *knowing*), that this "spiritual presence" is, in fact, Who I Am. And as I said previously, if it is Who I Am, then it must be able to be used as an integral part of my day-to-day experience—a fundamental tool in the process of creating my life.

So this experience allowed me to move from *hope* to *faith* to *knowing* about the fact that my reason for coming to the planet is in fact a *spiritual one*—and that every single thing that occurs in my life can be used to serve the Agenda of my Soul. And I think that the *point of intersection* is when the day-to-day living of our lives becomes a down-to-Earth physical expression of the spiritual beings that we are. In other words, *when the body becomes a vehicle for the soul,* just as the soul uses the body as a means to express and to demonstrate who and what it really is.

Is this correct? What are your thoughts, Neale?

I really have not been able to stop thinking about this. I mean, it's exciting. And empowering. *And it just makes so much sense.*

NEALE: Let's talk about two things.

First of all, yes, that is true—we are larger than our physical bodies. This is why the word metaphysical is used. *Meta,* meaning "larger than," or "greater than." So we are, in fact, *meta*-physical creatures. And nothing, I'm sure, would bring that more dramatically to one's consciousness than seeing a cadaver, or, for that matter, seeing a person on an operating table undergoing open heart surgery. So I can see how that would be very striking and very dramatic and very clear and present evidence that we are *meta*-physical and not just physical.

But let's get back to *hope, faith,* and *knowing.* The question that comes before anyone who's having a difficult time moving from hope to faith to knowing is, "What are we hoping? What are we having faith in? And what are we knowing?"

It's difficult for people to move to a place of knowing if what they are trying to know is that everything that they are desiring to experience in their life is going to happen. And that it's going to happen, furthermore, in precisely the way that they have thought to make it manifest.

I think there's a danger in the New Thought Community of believing in the Power of Personal Creation to the degree that we begin to feel that if something has not been made manifest in our reality, as we have sought to cause it to be, that we have somehow failed, that we have become "Spiritual Failures." That we're not "doing it right."

It would be a mistake, I think, for us to assume—for people to assume, much less to actually believe—that what they wish to see manifest in their lives, what they fervently desire to produce as outcomes in their physical reality, will occur without a doubt.

If people believe that it will occur without a doubt, should it not occur, they will then begin searching deeply for the reason. Why didn't it occur? And again, to repeat myself, they will no doubt make themselves wrong—I've seen metaphysical students do this—they'll make themselves wrong. "Well, I must not be doing it right." Or, worse, they'll go to a place of "This is all hogwash. I should have known from the beginning it was too good to be true!" So they'll throw the baby out with the bathwater. *Because they don't fully understand the process of manifestation, and what it is that we are trying to know.*

Through my 71 years on this planet I have come to understand that what we are well-advised to seek to know is not that whatever we call forth and whatever we command of the Universe will magically show up in our lives, whether it's that new red convertible, or the perfect life mate, or the exact income that we need, or any other occurrence or miracle that we are seeking to create. Not that that outcome will occur without fail in our lives, but rather, what we are well-advised to know is that the right and perfect outcome—*whatever it is*—will occur.

Those are two entirely different things.

And most of the New Thought Teachers do not teach what I've just said. Rather, they try to convince people that if they can move from *hoping* that something will be made manifest, to having *faith* that something will be made manifest, to *knowing* that something will be made manifest, then it *will be* made manifest. Even if it should be *not* in harmony with the Agenda of your Soul.

To use my own life as a particular example, a couple of times in my life—three or four times, actually—I have earnestly wanted particular things to occur. I think two or three of those four times had to do with my career.

I absolutely had the talent to become a nationally syndicated newspaper writer. And when I was working for a local newspaper in Annapolis, Maryland, I watched people in the newsroom being offered jobs at larger newspapers—at the Baltimore and Washington major metropolitan newspapers—and one person was even offered a job at the *New York Times.* He went right from our small paper straight to the big time. And I couldn't believe—not that these others had gotten the offer—I mean fair enough, God Bless 'em—*but that I hadn't.* And that they were, in a sense, passing me by. Especially since I had fervently hoped that I would one day get to be a reporter for the *New York Times.* I was a young man then, in my twenties, and I thought I deserved to have that kind of a break. *It didn't happen.*

The second time that I had that experience was when I was a talk show host on the radio and, likewise, I felt that I should be able to rise to the ranks of the best and highest paid and most widely known radio talk show hosts in America. The left wing version of the right wing guy, Rush Limbaugh, and I could be, you know, his left wing counterpoint. But I never got that opportunity, either.

And I could speak of other opportunities that didn't come to fruition in my life. But the point I'm making now is this: at 71, I realized that *if any of those things had occurred, I wouldn't be here now.*

So what I'm clear about is that *my soul takes a very clear-eyed look, if I could put it in human terms, at what it is that my mind is trying to manifest.* And if it's not in harmony with what my soul is aware would be a perfect physical manifestation, given my soul's individualized expression—given the *possibilities,* I should say, for the most dramatic and powerful individual expression of my soul's agenda (which has nothing to with a specific occupation, but with a state or states of Being)—if it's not in harmony with that, the energies in my life will work against that occurring.

But I noticed that as soon as I began doing things, and even hoping for things, that *served* the highest expression of the state of being that reflected my soul's agenda—that is, as soon as what my mind and heart wished for and sought to make manifest fell into *energetic harmony* with my soul's knowing of the highest possibility—*everything fell into place.*

I mean, literally, *everything fell into place!*

I sent a book to a publisher, and the odds of a totally unpublished, unheard of author sending a book to a publisher with the unbelievable title of *Conversations with God*—talk about pretentious!—the odds of a publisher saying, you know, "We gotta get this thing out, this guy's talking to God!". . . you've heard me say this in my speeches before, but the odds are one in a million—much less that the book would be published and begin selling so quickly, so rapidly, that within weeks of its publication it was on the *New York Times* Bestseller List, and stayed there for two and a half years. So everything began falling into place, and it's been falling into place ever since.

DR. COOPER: Yes, I know. So, Neale, I have a question about this . . .

You talk about your soul taking a very "clear-eyed look" at the circumstances in front of you to determine how it could best serve its agenda moving forward.

Many spiritual people would pose the question, "Is there a larger plan in place for us before we get to the planet? And, in moments such as these, is our soul 'redirecting us' toward some sort of 'larger plan'?"

NEALE: My understanding is that the answer is no. There's no "larger plan," in terms of an occupation or career. No larger plan that's been put into place for us, in the sense of: butcher, baker, candlestick maker. Our souls do not say, "You will be first baseman for the New York Yankees, you're going be a civil rights attorney in Alabama, and you're going be a doctor in Canada."

No. That kind of a plan does not exist, in my understanding.

The metaphor that I was given in *Conversations with God* is that we are given the paints on the palette that we choose from lifetime to lifetime. That is, *aspects of Divinity that we wish to express*, if you please. Purple, green, yellow, blue, red. *But we are not told how to paint the picture of our lives.*

So the canvas is ours, on which to paint the picture that we choose to paint. We have Free Will in that regard. But we are given the paints. So in this particular lifetime, it's pretty clear the gifts I've been given—what's been "put on my palette"—and also the challenges that have been placed before me. Patience, and so forth.

So all the colors were put on my palette, but God does not say, "This is what you shall paint, and you will paint it. It has to be a meadow, with the sun in the upper right corner, an orange flower in the lower left, and a tiny child off in the grass in the distance." So *no, there is no plan.*

DR. COOPER: I get it. So, when your soul "corrects course," so to speak—because you mentioned opportunities that you felt you should have had, based on your skill level, in writing and in radio talk show hosting that did not pan out—are you saying that you can see now, in retrospect, how perhaps this diversion was serving the truest expression of your soul's agenda?

NEALE: Not necessarily the truest expression of my soul's agenda, *Everyone's soul agenda is identical.*

It wasn't my soul's agenda that I would be the writer of a bestselling series of spiritual books. Everyone's soul agenda is identical, that's made very clear in *The Only Thing That Matters.* So it's not my soul's agenda that we're talking about here, but the best qualities, the energetic expression, that would most easily and rapidly and most powerfully facilitate the placing into the world of my soul's agenda through a particular avenue that would allow me to experience certain aspects—certain colors on my palette—that I came here to experience. To explain this more fully . . . I'm sure that two of the colors on my palette that I wanted to experience are *wisdom and clarity.* I've talked about this often.

DR. COOPER: Yes, I get that . . . But Neale, I'm still stuck on one point.

You mention that those paths you were interested in pursuing, be it in writing or in radio talk show hosting, did not pan out as you'd hoped, and that—if I heard you correctly—that this relates to it not being the optimum avenue to express those qualities (of wisdom and clarity, among other things) that your soul has come here to express in this lifetime.

So how does your soul know that that's not what you should be doing? How is it that those opportunities—you know, one might say they "failed to come to fruition," in the way you initially hoped they would—how does that relate to your soul "knowing" what you should be doing?

NEALE: Oh! Not what I "should" be doing, but what I have an opportunity to do—"this" as opposed to "that." How does the soul know anything? *The soul knows everything.*

How do you know when you meet a person, that this person would be good for you? How is "love at first sight" possible? *How does the soul know anything?* How do the mind and the soul combine and work together to come to an intuitive understanding of anything at all?

The question is larger than, "How does your soul know that a career choice may not be the best?" How does your soul know, "No, no, no— don't turn left, *turn right here.* I promise you, just turn right." So you make the right turn, in a strange city that you have no knowledge of, but you just have a *hunch,* and sure enough, that gets you exactly where you wanted to go. And everybody in the car applauds and says, "How did you know that?" And you say, "I have no idea how I knew that. I just felt like I needed to turn right and not left at that last corner."

How does the soul know anything? Big or small. Important or not important. And the answer is the soul, of course, knows everything. *There's nothing that's unclear to the soul.* So when the soul became aware of the mind's choice to become a syndicated radio talk show host, the soul said, "You know what, you can do what you want! Be a syndicated radio talk show host if you want to. I'm not going to stop you."

So the soul doesn't get in there and intervene and stop things from happening. It's not like the soul directs the activities or the outcomes of your life. But the energies that the soul transmits move through the body and the being—the three-part being that we are—in such a way that they are not the most harmonious with the energies that are incoming that offer us opportunities to step into a particular relation- ship, or occupation, or even live in a certain part of town, or in a certain house. Things just don't "feel" right. Things don't "fall into place" easily.

How many people have been house hunting and they walk into a house that they have found that is available and they walk in and they just turn around and they walk right out? And the real estate agent they're with says, "Whoa, whoa . . . you didn't even look at the—"

"I don't need to. I got as far as the living room and that's as far as I needed to go."

How many people—let's get even more miniscule in our examples— how many people go into their closet to pick out the perfect outfit for this important dinner, and they put it on, and they get as far as the front door, and they put their hand on the doorknob, and they say, "You know what? I can't do it!"? And they go back upstairs and completely change their outfit!

DR. COOPER: So it's about the *energetic harmony*. Is that what you're saying?

NEALE: Yes, that's a wonderful term. It is about the *energetic harmony*. It's about the energetic signature that *feels* to be more "in harmony" with the highest expression that the moment allows, making possible the completion of that portion of the Agenda of your Soul that is presenting itself right now.

DR. COOPER: How would one know that they are using the moment in a way that optimally serves the Agenda of the Soul?

NEALE: The answer to your question is that they would know by the *relative ease with which things are occurring.*

DR. COOPER: Hmmm.

NEALE: That's why most spiritual philosophers say, "Don't push the river."

DR. COOPER: Yes. "Row, row, row your boat, gently down the stream."

NEALE: Do not get out of the boat and start pushing the river! When things are not "in the flow," *pay attention to that.* And don't insist on having "your way." *Rather, watch life resolve itself in the process of Life Itself.*

The soul does not, and never will, *stand in the way* of any choice your mind wishes to make. But the soul can, and does, *pave the way* for that which is more in harmony with the agenda that you, yourself, set when you came into this lifetime.

To use our "palette" metaphor . . . let us say that the soul put a lot more green paint on your palette—tons of it—and very little beige or red or yellow. There's some there, but not a bunch. That's because the soul's agenda is for you to use green this lifetime more than any other color.

(Again, this is a metaphor. In my case, in terms of Qualities of Divinity—the "colors" of God—I am clear now that I had decided, at a soul level, to experience and express Wisdom and Clarity at a high level in this lifetime. That's a brave thing for me to say here, because it's very personal to my experience, and may sound even a bit arrogant to someone hearing it outside of the context of this conversation, but I'm going to say it out loud anyway, in order to clarify the point I've been making here.)

So now, using the framework of the above metaphor, you can see that I would not be *prohibited* from using my colors to paint a canvas with a cityscape full of buildings and skyscrapers, but that it would be a lot *easier* for me to paint a picture of an open grassy field leading into a forest.

Given the "paints" on my palette, my soul could see that radio talk show host, or New York newspaper writer, was not what I had the most harmonious energy for. My soul did not *stop* me from, or get in the way of, these career opportunities. It was just a matter of what was more in the Energy Flow. What was easier for me to do.

Life will always "go with the flow." What comes *easiest* to us is sometimes what we call our "natural talents." I had a talent for radio, yes, and a talent for journalism, too. But the biggest color on my palette made it easier for me to paint a different picture of my life.

And so our mind's opportunity in life is to, in a sense, get out of the way! Get our miniscule mental desires to be a famous talk show host, or a big city newspaper writer, off the table.

DR. COOPER: Got it!

NEALE: And sometimes we can't get it off the table *until we notice that it's not easily happening.* Or, that it's not happening *at all.*

So, the Spiritual Master is the one who notices what's happening and what's not happening. *And agrees with it all.* That's what caused Byron Katie to give us all the advice she offered in her fabulous book, *Loving What Is.*

DR. COOPER: I read that book. It's wonderful.

NEALE: That's the whole point of the book! The whole point of the book is to watch what's happening, *and to stop arguing with life.*

DR. COOPER: You honestly make things sound so beautiful, so simple, so perfect. As does Byron Katie!

I would like to touch briefly on a video interview of yours that I watched, Neale . . . one that addresses the Process of Personal Creation and the *Law of Attraction.*

You talk about how so many of us seek to manifest *external things*—and you reference the New Age movie *The Secret,* which shows people trying to "attract" the new sports car in the driveway, the new bicycle for the child, or the diamond necklace for the bodice. And the focus of almost the entire movie is on external materialistic things!

I love how you say, "If we supposedly hold this incredible power to attract anything into our lives, why wasn't even one minute—not one minute—of a nearly ninety-minute movie spent on *attracting the things that really matter? Like world peace? An end to suffering? A better me?"*

You point out in the video that there are plenty of people who *have* the external manifestations—be it the perfect job, the perfect mate, or the perfect house—*and who are still sad as hell.* And you go on to say that "there aren't many unhappy people walking around who are demonstrating patience, compassion, wisdom, understanding and love." *It just doesn't happen.*

So the most powerful message I took away from this video—if I understood it correctly—is that the *Law of Attraction* is not so much about manifesting things *exterior* to ourselves, but rather about demonstrating qualities *interior* to ourselves. In other words, it is about showing up in the world in such a way that *who we are being* becomes the richness and the treasure that we previously sought to experience through material possessions and accomplishments.

NEALE: I agree with all of that, and I would add, however, as a post-script to that, *that the two are not mutually exclusive.*

That is, one does not have to eschew, or step away from, or aban-don, any of one's exterior physical world ambitions, hopes, wishes, or dreams. *I believe that the approach that will make us profoundly happy is the one that you've just described, where we seek to demonstrate the highest and best within us with regard to how we express our humanity in the world at large, and our State of Being through that process.*

But I don't think that the two manifestation techniques are mutu-ally exclusive. That is, I think it's perfectly okay to visualize and seek to create, as well, certain physical world outcomes. But the Master is the one *who does it without attachment to results,* who doesn't *require* par-ticular desires to be made manifest in the particular form or shape that has been visualized or envisioned—or for them to be made manifest at all—in order to be happy, joyful, and content in life.

The Master is the one who says, "This, *or something better.*"

DR. COOPER: What a way to live! And in a sense *who you are being* actually magnetizes certain exterior-world outcomes in your life, doesn't it?

Yet my understanding is that the internal must precede the exter-nal . . .

NEALE: "Seek ye first the Kingdom of God, and all else shall be added unto you."

DR. COOPER: And as you said, Masters, it seems, are able to move through the world in a way that maintains detachment from results, such that whatever happens they understand is not only okay, *but actually in their best interest.*

NEALE: Precisely. And that is why I said, several minutes ago, that hope shifts to faith, and faith leaps to knowing, when what we have come to know *is that every outcome is perfect;* that perfection is being made manifest in and through our lives in every moment, *however it is appearing.* And that, given Who We Are as Spiritual Entities, anything *other* than perfection would be impossible. Nothing that happens to us is imperfect in any way. Peace arises out of seeing and embracing this immutable truth.

I notice that was one of the major spiritual principles in the very first book, in the very first couple hundred pages of the 3,000 pages of the *Conversations with God* dialogues. Book One offered us three words that I will never forget. They struck me when I saw them the first time.

"See the perfection."

Peace comes from *seeing the perfection.*

DR. COOPER: That's beautiful. Those three words.

NEALE: Well, they changed my life.

And not that I practice it all the time, because there are times when I simply get into my "local self," my "smaller self," and I don't see the perfection of what's going on right now. I can't figure it out. But there are also times when I do—or rather, when I stop *trying* to "figure it out" and just accept it as true—and those times are increasing, experienced by me more often these days than not.

Interestingly enough, some people think of me now as sometimes being detached and dissociated from what's going on around me, because I don't get into the "dramas" of life nearly as much as I used to. I still do now and then, but not nearly as much as I used to. So people say, "Well, he's getting older, and he's become more 'detached.'"

Well, it's not my age, I don't think. It's just that I've finally come to clarity—I could have come to this clarity when I was 33 as well. You don't have to be 71 to get here, it just took me that long—but I have come to the clarity that *seeing the perfection of whatever is occurring is a profound pathway to peace.*

But even more than that, even more than a pathway to peace, it is as well an extraordinarily effective tool in manifesting the next best physical expression in my exterior world. Because then I do not become one who is *resisting* what is occurring.

You see, "What you resist persists, and what you look at disappears. That is, it ceases to have its illusory form, and we see it for what it really is." Ah! The perfect opportunity for me to announce and declare, to express and fulfill, to become and to experience Who I Really Am.

So I say, *Thank You, God.*

And I move from anger and frustration and resentment and resistance to gratitude. Actually, to *gratitude.*

DR. COOPER: You often say the best prayer is one of *gratitude in advance that the perfect solution is already on its way.*

NEALE: Yes. My favorite prayer is: *Thank you, God, for helping me to understand that this problem has already been solved for me.* I have used that little prayer many times in my life.

But it always doubles back to: *What am I doing here? What is my purpose for even being alive?*

So what we *hope* for, and what we have *faith* about, and what we come to *know*, is that each moment of our life is co-created by the lot of us, and placed before each of us individually in the perfect way, allowing Divinity itself to be made manifest through us, and to be observed through the singular and collective experience of humanity.

So when we talk about the connection between physicality and spirituality, we notice that the point of connection between them is the point where *the agenda of both is identical.*

That's when we know that the "physical" us and the "spiritual" us have made a connection. *It's when the agenda of both is identical.*

DR. COOPER: Thank you for that, Neale.

Earlier you were talking about how we will "know we are on the right track" when we feel that sense of *energetic harmony.* That is, when the path we are on seems to flow a little more easily, if I could put it that way.

So just to make this applicable to us in a day-to-day, on-the-ground kind of way, are you saying that we will know we have reached the "point of intersection" when we begin to feel that sense of ease in our lives—as opposed to a sense of anxiety, or stress, or the subtle feeling that something is a little "off"?

Are you saying that when we hit this point we will experience smooth sailing? For the most part, anyway. That perhaps, at last, we will begin to truly *see the perfection?*

Is this how we will know?

NEALE: That's one sure way to know. Another way that we know, that I know, is when I feel *selfless.* That is, when I take myself out of the picture. And I move toward, and invite the Universe to provide for me, the highest and best good for all concerned. And when I remove myself from the scenario, and wish for, or pray for, or hope for, or have faith in, or *know* that the highest and best good *for all* will be served. That's the second way that I can find inner peace within me.

I simply take my personal desires, my personal hopes, wishes, and dreams, off the table, *except to the degree that they serve the highest good for all concerned.*

And I've done that a number of times in my life. I've actually made the prayer, I've actually said to God, "If it serves the highest good for all concerned, may this happen." Whatever the particular thing was.

And you know, I can recall a number of key points in my life when I invoked that prayer, and suddenly all the tension, all the stress, around the particular circumstance that I was involved in melted away. *It just melted away* as soon as I took myself and my own personal desires out of the picture.

And I am reminded of—not that I am a saint about it—but I am reminded of the words, which I thought of later . . . not before, but later . . . I've realized, *Oh my gosh, that's exactly what Christ said!* In the garden of Gethsemane he said: "Father, would that this cup pass from my lips. Yet not my will, but Thine."

And in that moment he released all opposition to anything that was happening, and found a place of peace within once again.

DR. COOPER: What powerful words! It reminds me of the book *The Only Thing That Matters,* which comes to the simple, yet profound, conclusion that the only thing that matters is *what one desires.* Yet this comment must be interpreted with careful attention to the spiritual nuance, for worry it may be misunderstood. This is because it is not referring to the small personal desires of any individual ego, but rather to the larger One. It is in this sense that the only thing that matters is what One desires.

NEALE: That is, what God desires. God being the "One" that we are talking about.

DR. COOPER: And in truth, *We Are All One.* This is, in fact, the most fundamental message that the New Spirituality is seeking to convey to today's people. *That everything is One Thing.* And that we are all part of the One Thing That Is. In considering the words "what one desires," we are, in fact, considering the sum total wishes and desires of All of Humanity and, more broadly, of All of Life.

So it seems to me that we can cease opposing the moment when we understand that whatever is occurring is occurring precisely because it serves the Larger Agenda of Life. That is, all things align with "what one desires," and it is simply a matter of shifting our smaller personal desires to be in alignment with the larger desires of All of Life.

NEALE: Capital O on the "one" . . . *what One desires.*

DR. COOPER: Absolutely! And the more years I spend immersed in your work, Neale, the more I have started to know and to deeply understand that *what serves me is what serves others.* That is, my personal fulfillment has become less and less about my individual story, and more and more about how it serves the larger agenda of people, in alignment with the concept *We Are All One.*

This is why I seek to no longer work solely as a physician, despite the fact that many people would view that as a "successful career path," with nothing to question or change. But I am compelled to do something different . . . Something that, for me, resonates more fully with what I want to contribute to the planet.

And that is to offer healing not just physically, but spiritually . . .

To be a doctor not just of the body, but of the soul . . .

And to care not only about my individual soul, but about the soul of all of humanity. The soul of the planet. And the soul of life—which is essentially facilitating the expression of God through every one of us.

I mean, with the degree to which you have changed my life, Neale, how could I not deeply desire to do the same for others?

NEALE: That is excellent. But let me add something here, if I may. I know what you mean, I have a sense of where you are coming from, when you say that you seek to be a doctor not just of the body, but of the soul. But just so that readers don't become confused, let me make it clear to everyone what I know is clear to you—that the human soul does not now, and will never, require "healing."

A "doctor of the soul" would not, therefore, care *for* the soul, but would care *about* the soul, just as you have said. I think it's important to make that distinction. Because you care *about* the soul—not just the soul of individuals, but as you've expressed it, the soul of the planet, and of life—I see you doing things in the future that offer an individual's body and the mind, our planet, and life itself, what one might call "Soul Medicine."

A Physician of the Soul can be a brand new category of humans who create a whole new level of well-being. Your job will be to bring the consciousness and the awareness of the soul to the whole human being. It will be to not only *describe* where spirituality and physicality meet (which many members of the traditional clergy attempt to do), but to *produce* that outcome, to *generate* that result, *metaphysically*, as an experience and not merely a theory, in Life as lived by members of our species.

And so, doctor, as a Physician of the Soul, bring to everyone whose life you touch the wonderful words of Rumi, the 13th century Sufi mystic:

Wherever you stand, bring the soul to that place.

Chapter Four

DOCTORS AND DEATH:
When to Resuscitate?

DR. COOPER: As someone also in the traditional medical profession, there is something that I think is key for us to address in this book: our *fear of death.*

We just finished talking about the Process of Personal Creation and getting "in the flow of life" in terms of being on a path that is both more peaceful and more in alignment with the life we are seeking to create. Yet I think one of the biggest things that can hold us back in the process of creation is our *fear of death,* and our general unwillingness to address and explore it as a culture.

This is why I found it so empowering and so freeing to have had that experience in the cadaver lab. *Because I had the opportunity to see, before my very own eyes, that we are so much more than our bodies.* And this knowing enabled me to truly live in a more spiritual way. For when we are afraid to die, I believe we are, at some psychological level, *equally afraid to live.*

NEALE: There is no doubt about that.

DR. COOPER: So what I would like to ask you about, and talk about here, is: *How can we effectively move past our fear of death? Are there some practical suggestions for people around this?*

Having witnessed so much around life and death in my work in the hospital, one of the gifts I received is that I have almost ceased to doubt that something wonderful—the next grand and glorious opportunity—will present itself at the time of our "passing." I just have an intuitive trust that there is *so much more going on here than what meets the eye.*

Imagine someone who is blind, and has been blind since birth. If we did not tell them about all the things they were missing out on seeing, they would have no idea such things even existed! Similarly, if someone were born deaf, and we didn't describe to them the beautiful sound of an orchestra, or the melodious trickle of a stream, or the majestic crash of ocean waves, or the sweet sound of their loved one's voice, they, too, would have no idea what they were missing.

Scientifically, we believe that we have five senses, and we assume that these five senses encompass all there is to experience about life. Yet when one of these senses is missing, we miss out on a whole world of experience. *And we would not know we were missing out on it unless others told us about it.*

So to me it is clear that there is *more to life than meets the eye.* And I believe that death does not by any means imply an ending, in the strict sense of the word, but rather a new beginning upon which we have chosen to embark as the next phase of our Soul's Journey.

My "academic upbringing," however—having been "raised" by the medical profession, so to speak—has surrounded me with the viewpoint that *death is the worst outcome;* that we are to seek to avoid death at all costs. And that, in the absence of an Advance Directive, we would rather keep people alive well past the point where their body is "functional." That is, their quality of life may arguably be not worth living for, but we would rather keep them alive than accept death as the outcome. And something just seems so wrong to me about this.

NEALE: Brit, I know I'm not answering your main question, but I have something important I want to say here.

The doctor should not be the one to make that decision.

So what I want you to know is that the medical profession's insistence that, in the absence of an Advance Directive, life shall be the primary priority is *exactly correct.*

No doctor in any operating room, or in any procedure whatsoever, should have the moral authority, or the spiritual authority, to say, "Well, you know what, death is just as good as life in this case, and their quality of life may not be hardly any good at all if we resuscitate this person, or find some miracle way to keep him alive. So let's just let him die. Because, in my judgment, I've made an assessment that he'd be better off dead." That should not be an assessment made by a physician, or someone other than the person or his or her representative.

So the problem is not that the doctors and the medical profession are biased in favor of continuing life. The problem is that when the person is alive and aware enough to make their own decision that they no longer choose to continue living in a certain way (having had their lives saved by a doctor), they are not given the authority over their own life that the *doctor* would have over their life. That is, they are given *less authority* once they get out of the operating room and decide, "You know what, thanks for saving my life, but I don't want to live this way for the rest of my life. I want to die." They have less authority than the doctor had!

Doctors get to make life or death choices in those moments, *but the patient does not.*

So the problem is not that the doctor is choosing life, and doing everything the medical profession can bring to bear in order to continue a person's life. That isn't the issue! They *should*, rightly, continue a person's life in the absence of an Advance Directive, precisely so that the *person involved* could make *their own decision* about whether they want to live or die with a reduced quality of life—or at least have their medical or health care representative, presumably someone close to them, make that decision.

After doctors do the best they can to keep the person alive (and supposing they're successful and the person survives, even though their quality of life is greatly reduced), then they can say to that person, "Do you choose to continue living this way? Or, do you choose to do the thing that we call on this Earth 'die'? Do you choose to end this particular physical life?"

And if that person says "yes," then doctor-assisted suicide should be permitted. And the very same medical profession that saved that person's life should be able to permit the person or his or her representative to choose death. Because the reason we're saving the person's life in such critical moments *is to give them a choice!* Not that we, as doctors, or more broadly as a society, are going to make the choice for them.

So we rightly *should* keep them alive, to preserve the choice for *them*, to let *them* decide what "quality of life" *they* feel is sufficient. Once they're fully revived and fully thought-functional (or have representatives who are), then we should say, "Do you want to live in this iron lung for the rest of your life? Do you want to live paralyzed from the neck down for the rest of your life? Do you want to live with a feeding tube? Do you want to live with a colostomy bag? I mean, how do you want to . . ." And if the person says, "You know what, I don't want to do this, I'm out!", then the same medical profession should say, "Fair enough. Can't blame you a bit. And here, take these pills and fall into a gentle sleep tonight, and we'll remove your body in the morning."

So that's where the problem is. We don't give people—individual human beings—the authority over their *own lives* that we actually give doctors over those lives.

But if I'm in an operating room and I don't have an Advance Directive that says, you know, "No unusual efforts should be made to keep me alive"—if I don't have an Advance Directive . . . you're doggone right, I want the doctor to do what he can to save my life! I don't want *him or her* to assume that I would rather die. It's not her choice to make. It's mine!

So I want the medical profession to bring all the miracles of modern medicine to bear to keep me alive. Then I get to say, "You know what," to my family and my loved ones, and to my doctor, "I'm going to choose to die now."

Like that lady in the news recently. I forgot who she was, but she actually announced publicly—she told the papers and the news media— the day of her death. She chose the day and the time, and she and her family had their celebration, and she said goodbye to her loved ones, then took the medication and slept into her death.

DR. COOPER: Yes, I know the story. That was Brittany Maynard, a young 29-year-old woman who was diagnosed with a terminal brain tumor called a "glioblastoma."[5]

She would have preferred for her life to go on had she been perfectly healthy (she made it clear that she did not wish to die) but, given that there was no cure available to her, she chose to give herself six months to spend with her loved ones and then to die (as permitted by Oregon's *Death with Dignity Act*).

She explained that she preferred this option of a "death with dignity" rather than to suffer the debilitating consequences of the brain tumor that would eventually take her life.

Brittany Maynard's story captured a lot of media attention, and I think the blessing in this young woman's choice is that it opened the world's eyes to an alternate way of looking at death and dying. *It provided a real-life account of how it would look to give the patient the choice.*

NEALE: Yes. And that's the way it should be. In an advanced, intelligent civilization, *that is, of course, the way it should be.*

We depend on the medical profession to use every miracle at its disposal to keep us alive, precisely so that we can make our own decision about it.

DR. COOPER: I got it!

NEALE: And I'm saying that so often—I've said it five times now—so you can rearrange your thinking.

DR. COOPER: And save you, Neale?

NEALE: Of course! If I can't depend on you . . .

You know, it's not your job to decide what's best for me! It's my job. Your job is to keep me alive, so that I can make that decision! So I want you to rearrange your thinking, so that you won't be so negative about, "Well, the medical profession shouldn't be so biased in favor of extending life." Of course it should! That's what medicine's about! *To give us the freedom.*

The sadness is that modern life has *not* given human beings the freedom. The medical profession saves a person's life, then that person's trapped by society, by actual laws that stop us from making our own choices. That's where the problem is.

DR. COOPER: That makes so much sense. And I totally agree. Thank you for that.

NEALE: Well, I'm telling you right now if I'm in my family room in my house and you happen to be visiting me and I have a sudden stroke sitting in the chair, while you're sitting across the room, I'm not going to let you decide, "Well, you know what? He's had a good life. He's probably going to wake up from this stroke and not even be able to move, he'll be unable to speak, he'll be a vegetable. I'll just let him die."

No, no, no!

I'm gonna depend on you sitting there to do whatever you can do to keep me alive! That's why you're a doctor!

DR. COOPER: Yes, yes! And I will!

NEALE: Now, getting back to your earlier comment around the benefit of releasing our fear of death . . . *it is profoundly true.*

Dr. Elisabeth Kübler-Ross was the first person I heard that from. She put it in one simple sentence. One simple sentence! She said in her delightful heavy Swiss accent, *"When you are not afraid of dying, you are not afraid of living."* She captured all that wisdom in about twelve words.

So to sum it up, I would say this: The individual person is well-advised not to be afraid of death. But *doctors* should *well* be afraid of their patients dying! Because if they are not afraid of their patients dying, and if they do not do everything they can do to *stop* their patients from dying, their patients won't have the option of making the choice they wish to make with regard to life and death. That's not the doctor's decision to make.

DR. COOPER: I agree.

NEALE: Unless there's an Advance Directive that says "No extraordinary measures," or words to that effect. That's a whole different story. But if I don't have an Advance Directive, believe me, I'm depending on that guy in the operating room to perform whatever miracle he has to perform to keep me alive!

DR. COOPER: For sure!

And if I'm sitting across from you and you have something happen, I'll do everything I can to keep you alive!

NEALE: Oh good! So you won't think that you're wrongly "biased" in favor of life?

Good. I'm glad you said that. That makes me feel much more confident.

Chapter Five

THE JOURNEY OF THE SOUL:
What Happens At The End

DR. COOPER: I think it's important we touch on the idea of *Oneness* in this book. Not only because it is one of the most powerful and transformative spiritual concepts, but also because if Medicine has taught me anything, it has showed me with astonishing clarity the truth of our Oneness.

NEALE: It is one concept that, if fully embraced and understood, *would single-handedly change the world.*

DR. COOPER: It absolutely is. I can't tell you how many patients I have sat at the bedside with, in the final moments of their lives, who have had moments of great wisdom and profound insight into what matters. At the end of their lives, they have come to see that *the things that matter most in life all relate back to our Oneness*—be it our relationships with others, the services we have given to humanity, and our connection to the world at large.

And patients have actually shared this with me! They have shared their "pearls of wisdom" into what matters, in hopes that I could benefit sooner rather than later in my life. And I have been extremely grateful for this. It has certainly been one of the gifts of working in the medical profession.

NEALE: There's a very important and fundamental reason why the first impulse—or perhaps, to reframe it, the final impulse, the last impulse—that people feel when they are faced with the final moments of their lives, and they know it consciously, there's a fundamental reason why that final impulse is the impulse to express their remembrance that the most wonderful moments of their life were the moments when they experienced Oneness.

And there's a fundamental reason why whenever we talk to people who are in the final moments of their life, and they know it, there's a fundamental reason why they say those things.

And the reason is that the basic instinct . . . people think that the basic instinct is survival, but it is not. The basic instinct is the impulse toward Divinity. And that impulse can be defined as the experience of Oneness, or Unity—the Unity of All Things.

It is *instinctive* for human beings to seek the experience of Unity and Oneness with All of Life—not just with other people, by the way, not just with other human beings, but with All of Life.

We pass a garden and we want to put our nose in the lilacs. We want to be just part of that experience! We look up at a night sky and we yearn, we long—almost sometimes with an aching in our heart—to somehow merge with those diamonds in the sky. And even from this great distance, from millions of light years away, we can still *feel the Unity* of being One with the night sky, and there's not a person alive who has not felt that.

DR. COOPER: It's so true. I love looking up at the night stars!

NEALE: Yes. *And it's the experience of everyone.*

And similarly, some people are drawn to the sea, and they'll stand silently at the seashore—I don't know a person of any age who hasn't spent at least three minutes of their life standing all alone, silently, where they can hear the roar of the ocean as it smashes on the shoreline, and even maybe catch a bit of the water with their feet in the sand. And they *feel* that sense, as the ocean crashes in on them, that they are part of the whole milieu of life.

And as the water recedes back into the ocean itself, having washed the beach with each incoming wave, as it returns to itself, *a part of us goes with it.* And we *feel* that. I'm not making that up! That's not just a poetic thing to say. *We actually feel a part of ourselves going back to the ocean.*

Which is why we stand there and allow ourselves to have the experience over and over again.

And I've had that experience of standing on a seashore and watching the ocean come in and crash in on the beach and wash back out again, *taking an aspect of me with it.*

DR. COOPER: It's so true—there is that presence that washes over us in moments like that, *inviting us to become one with it.* And of course we *are* one with it—it is simply a matter of seeing it, knowing it, and including it as an aspect of our awareness.

I find it interesting that many people are called to the water—or called to Nature in general—during times of struggle and stress in their lives. It is almost as if we know that when our smaller selves, our "ego selves," get lost and caught up in the rat race of day-to-day life, that returning to Nature allows us to reconnect with our larger selves—*the piece of ourselves that is eternally connected to All of Life.* And having that reminder, that connection with the natural world, helps us to reclaim the peace, the truth, and the joy that is a part of our essential nature.

I remember personally going through a stressful time in my life, about a year ago. I felt a powerful pull to go down to the beach at night and to watch the sunset, whenever I had time to, and whenever I could. And I actually remember thinking to myself in those moments, "Gosh, I wonder if I am called back to the ocean, and back to the sunset, *to see and to remember a piece of myself.*" And it sounds like this is true, from what you just said!

It was almost like an evening "date" to go and say hello to my soul again! To return to the Oneness—*and in doing so, to remember Who I Am.*

NEALE: Not only that, my dear, not only that. Those are the magical moments that are easy to identify. But the fact of the matter is that *every moment in life is designed to call you back to yourself.* You are standing at the ocean shore every moment of your life.

DR. COOPER: Yes!

NEALE: Not just when the moments that are so magical you can't miss them, but when the moments are part of every single element of your life. Nothing occurs in life that is not a "street sign" pointing back Home.

DR. COOPER: Why then do you think it's difficult for many people to see that, or to implement that in their lives? To see that every moment, and every situation, is an opportunity to "return home"?

NEALE: *Because all of our lives we've been told the Story of Separation.*

It starts with a Separation Theology, which says that God's over there and we're over here, and we hear it everywhere! Even if we don't buy it, even if we don't believe it, even if we don't have it as our personal theology, *we hear it everywhere!*

And the Separation Theology produces a Separation Cosmology. It simply creates a cosmological view of things that says we live in an environment where everything is separate from everything else.

And that Separation Cosmology produces, inevitably, a Separation Psychology—a psychological holding of life that says that I'm over here, and everyone else is over there, and I'm separate from everyone else. My longing to be otherwise notwithstanding, I'm separate from everything else. And that Separation Psychology produces all kinds of psychoses!

As every psychiatrist will tell you, and every psychologist as well, that Separation Psychology inevitably produces a Separation Sociology. That is, an entire society that imagines itself to be separate from other societies. And "better"—not just separate, but "better than." I'm better because I'm white. I'm better because I'm black. I'm better because I'm gay. I'm better because I'm straight. I'm better because I'm male. I'm better because I'm female. I'm better because I'm tall. I'm better because I'm short.

And that Separation Sociology inevitably produces a Separation Pathology. *Pathological behaviors of self-destruction.* Observable on our planet everywhere you look, across thousands of years.

That's the answer to your question "why"! It's because we have been immersed in a Separation Theology, which produces a Separation Cosmology, then a Separation Psychology, then a Separation Sociology, then a Separation Pathology.

The pathway is quite clear.

And the reason that we find it so hard to follow the instinctive call to rejoin the All—say, that's my poem for the day!—*the instinctive call to rejoin the All!* The reason we have difficulty doing this is that everything in our lives has pointed us in the opposite direction, producing the outcomes I just gave you. So it's not a surprise to me. It's not a surprise to me that we have a difficult time embracing our Unity, except at the end of our life, when we realize that, in fact, *our life itself has proven it, over and over again.*

We think back on the days and times of our life, and we notice then, just as we are ending our life, that the only truly meaningful moments were the moments in which we experienced our Oneness. Not just with other people, but with the ocean, with the sunset, with the night sky, and with All of Life itself.

And not only does that dawn on us, not only is that made clear to us emotionally and psychologically at the moment of our Death because of the glorious and happy joyous memories, but it also overcomes us at the moment of our "Little Deaths"—the times in our life when meaningful relationships and experiences end.

And we experience it so fully, in such a present way, as our "Big Death" approaches because of the joyous and happy hopes that it is a harbinger—a signal of things to come. And we smell it like the fresh morning dew! "Ahhh! It's back to the Oneness I'm going to now! I know that I'm leaving *here*, but finally, finally—at last—my periodic 'aloneness' is over. Everyone who I have ever loved will be there! Everything I have ever deeply enjoyed will be enjoyed again! And the God that I have adored with such open heart and open arms will be welcoming *me* with open arms!

DR. COOPER: I get it! That is beautiful. So it is not only a recollection of the most meaningful moments of our lives, but also a *foreshadowing* that the Oneness is and will always continue to be the truth of Who We Are.

It really makes me wish more people could come to these realizations sooner in life . . . and that we could *all* experience first-hand evidence of our Oneness with All of Life, and with God, without having to get to our deathbed to know that it's true. I mean, it really surprises me how such a popular spiritual message—*We Are All One*—can be so readily embraced *conceptually*, but can be such a challenge to live by *experientially*.

That doesn't surprise you at all?

NEALE: It doesn't surprise me, given what I know about life.

Fear is a powerful emotion. It's the second most powerful emotion, next to its parent—which is Love. All Fear is born of Love, of course. But Fear is a very, very powerful emotion. So I'm not surprised, because even as we yearn for the sloughing off of our individual and separate identity, for our experience of Oneness, *we fear it.*

And that is the Divine Dichotomy. That is what I call the Supreme Irony. That even as the average human being yearns to merge back with the Oneness and seeks to never know loneliness again, in the self-same moment *it fears the loss of its identity.*

DR. COOPER: So it is fearing that it will lose its sense of self if it embraces Oneness?

NEALE: Yes. That it will lose its sense of *individuation.* Yet the Great Promise of God is that this will not happen. That even when you merge back into the All, that is not your eternal state. The eternal state is the experience and the expression of our individuated soul.

Now the Great Promise of God is *that we will not lose our sense of self simply because we merge with the All.* Because the process of merging with the All is not eternal.

That is, we merge with the All, and it is a *temporary process.* And what occurs, ultimately, is that we *emerge.* Firstly we merge *into*, and then we emerge *from*, The All, and return again to the individuated identity of the soul.

And then we are allowed to decide if we wish to continue on the expression of physical life in the identity most recently embraced—in my present case, as Neale—and if that's what's so, then we literally "return to life." We come back to life, whether we're on the operating table or whether we're clinically dead in some other way, or whatever, we come back to life as who we have been.

We can also make the decision to "stay dead," so to speak; to stay on the other side, to continue our Spiritual Journey, in which case we become then aware, in the Realm of the Absolute, of all the identities we have ever expressed as—that we have ever embraced. And we come to know all those identities—that is, we meet all of our other so-called "selves." *We experience ourselves as every aspect and expression of Divinity that we have ever embraced, throughout all of time.*

By the way, not just those we have embraced in what we call, in our illusion, the "past," but those we are *going* to embrace in what we call, in our illusion, the "future."

That is, we know ourselves as all of our selves. And we get so excited! That is, by the way, what brings us back to physical life.

People have often asked me, *If heaven is so wonderful, why do we come back to Earth?* I've had some people say to me, "I don't want any more incarnations, I'm done!"

But I can tell you that I've been reliably informed that when we get back to the Realm of the Spiritual, we are made aware of—we meet up again, if I could put it that way, with—all the selves we ever have been, *or ever will be!* And our next future self is so exciting to us! It's so thrilling to us!

We don't "see in the future" in the sense of knowing exactly what will happen to that Future Self. This would suggest Predestination, and such a thing does not exist. But we *do* see *all the possibilities,* all of the *endless and exciting choices,* that our Future Self will have placed before it. So that we decide, of *course,* to come back into physicality to experience that particular incarnation, and to confront all those choices. Or, to experience *another version* of our *present* incarnation—for the exact same reason.

So, you know, this all gets wonderfully sophisticated and complex—people have heard me talk of these things and they've said, "You've got a great imagination, Neale, but you know, this is really starting to get pretty weird." At which point I quote my wonderful friend of the soul, William Shakespeare.

It was Bill who said: *There are more things in Heaven and Earth, Horatio, than are dreamt of in your philosophy.*

DR. COOPER: I have a question, then.

You say that when we "cross over," and do the thing called "die," all of our "selves," past, present, and future, will be known to us. And we will find this remarkably exciting, and—

NEALE: Especially the future ones, yes!

DR. COOPER: Yes! So my question is: *What is the difference between an Individual Soul and the "One Soul"?*

Have we, at some point, been every single person who has ever lived and who ever will live, past, present, and future? Or, is there a distinction?

Like when people consider the notion of "past lives," is it correct to say I've had 647 past lives, just to give an example? Or, is it, in fact, true that I am every single thing in the cosmos, which would imply that I have had infinite lives and that there is no distinction between myself and any other person or being or thing.

So my question is: *Am I the All of It, experiencing Itself in all of its parts simultaneously? Or, am I a discrete part?*

NEALE: Yes . . .

DR. COOPER: Or, am I both, experiencing life as a Divine Dichotomy?

NEALE: The answer is Yes.
  (Laughs.)
  When you merge with The All, you experience the part of yourself that is The Only Thing There Is. You experience yourself as everyone and everything that ever was, or is now, and ever will be. *And that is, in fact, the point of merging*. And you get to experience that. You get to experience that not only are you coming Home, but you *are* Home.

  You are All There Is, All There Ever Was, and All There Ever Will Be, including every person who's ever lived. And, for that matter, every *thing* that has ever been made manifest at any level of physicality. You experience that you are Everything. All Of It. That there is Only One Thing, and that this thing is You. In short, you experience your True Identity, as God.

  Then you emerge again, in a sense. To borrow a phrase, you are "born again"—you emerge from the One, and are then given the opportunity to remember and to foresee both, to remember and to foresee all of the particular individuations that the Singularity you now express as has embraced, or will embrace, in the eternal and only moment, called Now.

DR. COOPER: So in this lifetime, if I'm interacting with someone, or looking into a loved one's eyes, am I in fact looking into a piece of myself?

NEALE: Of course! Absolutely! In the sense that we are all part of The Only Thing There Is, in the sense that we are all waves on the same ocean, yes, of course.

And that's why we can't look into anyone else's eyes for very long, even someone that we deeply love. There's a limit to how long we can look into someone's eyes when we're in human form, because ultimately *we see ourselves there.*

And that insight—literally "in sight," to see into oneself, by looking into the eyes of another—is at once both disarming and so producing of absolute bliss that it's almost more than we can bear.

It's the reason why we actually have to look away from each other. If we look at each other for too long, . . . and for some people it would be longer than others . . . but no one can hold that stare for very long, because we begin to see ourselves, *and we fall in love with ourselves again.*

And when we see ourselves in the other, we also come to a place of unconditional love, because we are seeing ourselves *as* the other. Everything that the other has ever done—wonderful things and not so wonderful things—are suddenly completely and totally understood. Because we see that it is identical in some basic form to everything that we have ever done.

DR. COOPER: I love the idea that, as we look into someone's eyes, if we look long enough we will *see ourselves there.* It is the "human gateway" into the experience of Oneness!

As you just said, it is the moment in which complete forgiveness and understanding become not only possible, but *inevitable.* Because as we look into another's eyes and *truly begin to see ourselves there,* we immediately see that whatever they may have done to us or for us, we have done to or for another to some degree as well. And so our entire "viewpoint" is altered dramatically!

And gosh, if that doesn't cause us to take a double-take on any sort of judgment we may have inflicted, and if it doesn't immediately open us to a space of overwhelming compassion and understanding, then I don't know what would.

But getting back to the Oneness idea, I have read a lot both in the CwG books as well as in other spiritual literature about how embracing the idea of Oneness would profoundly alter life on the planet for the better. And about how, if we saw each other as all members of the same "human family," and began sharing and demonstrating this truth through our choices and actions, the state of our world could be transformed literally overnight! And I see the power and the importance of this message.

However, what I'm really interested in focusing on here is how we can incorporate the concept of Oneness into our *individual lives,* and what impact it would have if we did. To me, this is where the question is at . . . because in order to create change on a global scale, we must first consider how it would look in our individual lives.

Am I making sense here?

NEALE: Yes, of course you are.

DR. COOPER: So I'm very curious what your thoughts are on how can we embrace Oneness more in our own lives.

NEALE: By calling it to mind deliberately.

By asking ourselves certain questions, and by using certain mental "tricks," I want to say, or mental tools.

One of my favorite mental tools is the tool of "I Am." Most religions have shared with their followers the great statement that God is purported to have made at some point along the way: "I Am That I Am."

When I was a child I heard that in my Catholic Parochial School more than once. "I Am That I Am." Supposedly a statement applying to all things, a pronouncement of all truth, from God to humanity.

And I asked the priest in my catechism class, "What does that mean, I Am That I Am?" And he said, "I really can't tell you specifically and literally. It means broadly that God is everything, but the literal translation of that into those words . . . you know, I'm not sure I really understand how that gets there, how those words take us to that place of awareness."

And then I was invited by God, in my *Conversations with God,* to repeat that statement with regard to everything that I looked at. To once a week walk down the street for fifteen minutes and quietly say in my own mind, to no one else, just saying it to myself, with regard to everything upon which my eyes light: "I Am That."

"I Am That. I Am That. I Am That."

And I remember doing that once, just silently when I was walking down the street with a friend, actually. I didn't want to make a big issue of it, and I just did it in my mind, in my head. But she saw that I was preoccupied with something, and she finally said, "What are you doing? I don't understand . . . what are you doing?"

And I said, "Oh, I didn't realize it was that obvious. I'm just saying something to myself."

And she said, "Well, what are you saying to yourself?"

And I said, "Well I'm just saying 'I Am That. I Am That. I Am That. I am that beautiful flower across the street in the flower pot, I am that garbage truck going by, I am that beautiful French poodle with its tail wagging for its master, I am that other lady walking. I Am That'."

And my friend looked at me and she said, "Wow, you've really gone over the edge! You're really losing it, man. You're *not* that! You're you! Did this New Spirituality of yours make you think that you're not you anymore?"

I said, "No, no! I *am* that!"

She said, "No, you're not that!"

I said, "No, no, no, I *am* that, I AM!"

And then I heard what I just said.

I heard my own voice. "I am that," I was insisting. "I am that, *I am!*" And then I realized that the Great Statement of God had been historically mistranslated. It had been, from the start, "mis-written"! *They forgot to put the comma in.* The place for the comma is, "I am that . . . (comma) . . . I am."

And then I understood.

So that's one tool that I use. Once a week I walk down the street or walk around the house for fifteen minutes and repeat to myself, in my own mind, "I Am That." *Whatever my eyes light upon.* And I don't reject it if it's ugly or doesn't seem pleasant, and I don't allow myself to feel somehow overblown in my own mind if it's something beautiful and wonderful. I just notice that I'm telling myself the truth about everything.

Now a second tool that I use is when I see anyone do anything—and this is not a once-a-week thing. I try to do this as often as I can during a regular day—when I observe what looks like another person behaving in a certain way.

This is particularly useful when their behavior is a little bit off-putting, but it can also be used when their behavior is attractive as well. I say in the moment that I observe the behavior of another, "There I go again. *There I go again.*" And then, by that means, I notice two things. One: I've done the same exact thing in my life that I see that person doing. And two: I'm doing it again in my life! Through that other person. Because there really is no Separation.

And so that's how I allow myself to feel "at one" with the other person. I often ask myself the question, "Have I ever experienced a part of me that's behaved in this exact same way?" And the answer inevitably comes back, yes. And then I have a physical experience of being one with that other.

And the third way, the third and final tool that I share with people about being able to bring that experience of Oneness forward, is by noticing that there have been times in my life when I have felt the *feeling* of another as if it were my own. And I can remember those times vividly.

There have been moments when I have been so empathic that I could actually feel the feelings of another as if I was feeling them, right then and there.

And that is not terribly unusual. All of us have those moments. But when I have those moments, I store them in my memory bank, in a special place that I return to when I'm feeling separate from another, or when I'm feeling the need or the desire to reconnect with my sense of Oneness.

Feelings are the language of the soul, and I've had many moments in my life when I have joined another in their feelings so completely that they might as well have been my own feelings. And then the Separation between us virtually disappears. Moments of great sadness, moments of great happiness, moments of great joy, moments of great victory, moments of defeat—I have shared those moments emotionally as if they were my own. I have not merely observed them, I have not merely witnessed them, I have actually *shared them*. I have felt them *simultaneously* with the other. All of us have had those kinds of shared experiences. And recalling those moments, and being on the lookout for them again, is another tool that I use when I want recall the experience of my Oneness with others.

DR. COOPER: With all of the practice you've had spiritually, how do you find your experience now, day-to-day, in terms of feeling Separation versus feeling Oneness?

NEALE: I'm feeling Separation probably 60 or 70 percent, maybe 80 percent of the time. And I'm feeling Oneness maybe 10 or 15 or 20 percent of the time . . . as opposed to how it used to be, when I felt Oneness about 2 percent of the time. So I think I've made huge strides.

But Mastery, of course, is feeling that experience of Oneness *all the time*. I'm not even close to that. But I'm heading there, and I'm increasing the number of moments in my life when I feel that. I can feel it increasing almost on a day-by-day basis.

So am I feeling more "at one" with another and with everything else in life than I did twenty years ago, before *Conversations with God?* Oh, my gosh, yes. Because in those days I really didn't experience that more than 2 or 3 percent of the time—when I had a particular moment of incredible, singular bliss. But not these days. Today I can experience that without necessarily having it be accompanied by, or be an intrinsic part of, some kind of transcendent moment.

DR. COOPER: Yes. I got it.

Well, thank you for those tools. I'm excited to try them!

Chapter Six

MEDICAL MIRACLES:
Are They Within Our Reach?

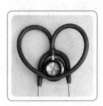

DR. COOPER: The concept of "medical miracles"—whether they exist and, if so, what increases one's chance of having a "miracle"—has been debated and discussed both in the medical and the spiritual literature. Yet the two have contrasting viewpoints.

Medical science holds the viewpoint that "miracles" are rare and out of our control; that they defy all logical understanding. Yet spiritual teachers across the globe have been saying otherwise for as far back as anyone can remember.

Still, no solid conclusions have been reached about medical miracles, and how they come about. It is certainly a topic that invites us to consider the very title of this book. For it seems to me that the *Intersection of the Physical and the Spiritual* would be the most likely realm from which a miracle could, and possibly would, emerge.

NEALE: Let's stop for a moment to define the word "miracle." Let's start off giving our readers a chance to understand . . . because "miracle" is a big word.

DR. COOPER: It is.

NEALE: I am holding, in my vocabulary, that a "miracle" is an event—and, in the context of this book, it's a medical event, or a health occurrence—that stands outside of, that runs against, all the odds of what would normally or usually occur in a circumstance surrounding a particular medical condition. That is, it defies the odds for sure, and it appears to be an occurrence that has no logical explanation from a strictly medical, from a traditional medical, point of view. So that's how I would define a miracle.

And, of course, we all know that they occur. Doctors are astonished and flummoxed and often shocked and surprised by certain turns of events that occur in the lives of their patients from time to time. So we have known throughout human history that miracles occur. As you just said, the question becomes: *Why, and how?*

DR. COOPER: Yes, it absolutely becomes *why,* and *how,* do miracles happen . . .

But before we delve into that, I have an important observation about the medical profession in general, and this is that the whole foundation of medical science is based on *probabilities.*

What I mean by this is that anytime a patient has a disease, technically we do not know what is going to happen. There is no hundred-percent guarantee that the person will get better, or get worse, or need surgery, or not need surgery, or live, or even die for that matter. *All we can offer the patient is our best guess as to what will occur next.*

It's really kind of a statistical way of looking at things. It's like saying, "Okay, 95 out of 100 patients with this illness are going to proceed in the following way." And the way in which medical treatments are designed is to try to group people in the most probable way in which their outcome will ensue.

What this means is two things. First of all, it means that "medical miracles" *have to exist* by virtue of the fact that we cannot logically (and scientifically) account for all possible outcomes. That is, if we are treating based on probabilities and the likelihood of certain outcomes occurring, there will be *by definition* a select few cases that are deemed "miracles" because the outcome was so unexpected it could never have been predicted or anticipated based on the medical research.

Secondly, though, and perhaps more importantly, it opens the question and the discussion around *what explains medical miracles?* Because the mystery behind "medical miracles" is not only that they are exceedingly rare, but perhaps more intriguingly that they are for the most part *utterly and completely unexplainable by modern medicine and science!* This is where the "spiritual door" opens, and invites us to consider a new perspective. We begin to ask what, in fact, could be responsible for such a drastic shift for the better in someone's state of health and wellbeing?

Anita Moorjani, author of *Dying To Be Me,* is an advocate for the idea that "miraculous healing" can occur at the behest of the soul.[6] Having been diagnosed with a terminal cancer, Moorjani experienced herself "dying" and "crossing over to the other side," only to realize that the journey of her soul was to come back to experience *life as a gift* (which she called "Heaven on Earth"), and to share her experience with others. She went on to write a bestselling book about it, which has certainly touched the lives of many, many people.

So to summarize what I'm trying to say here, *medicine is about predicting future outcomes based on past data and past outcomes*. It utilizes the mind to synthesize all of the previous data from similar cases in order to create an anticipated outcome, which is called the patient's "prognosis."

But nowhere in western medicine is there space for the soul. The soul, I believe, is open to all possible outcomes—even those that cannot be explained by past data, or by the so-called "most likely trajectory" of the illness. So it is completely understandable that there could be a spiritual underpinning to some of the most unexplainable outcomes that have so often been deemed "medical miracles."

This is precisely what happened for Anita Moorjani.

And I happen to believe that it can occur for anyone, *should it be what their soul absolutely and unequivocally desires.*

NEALE: It is entirely understandable that the medical profession would, at first blush, reject the idea of miracles as a "to-be-counted-on" occurrence in medical circumstances precisely because, while the medical profession admits and acknowledges that miracles do occur, such outcomes do not occur with sufficient reliability or predictability to satisfy any reasonable projection of expectation, to say nothing of literally a *scientific prognosis,* for a patient's future.

So precisely because the nature of miracles is that they're entirely unexpected, unpredictable, and inconsistent, doctors have to warn— and we, as authors of this book, need to warn our readers as well—not to look for or depend on miracles as their highest probability. We need to make it clear to the people who are reading this material that, while we agree that miracles occur, and that they're an observable part of humanity's experience of itself and have been, as we said, across thousands and thousands of years, we nevertheless don't want this chapter to give people false hope that there is some kind of a process—some kind of metaphysical or spiritual process—that is guaranteed to produce miracles routinely.

So that presents an interesting dichotomy! For us as writers, and for the people in the world. The Dichotomy is that at the same time that we say that miracles occur, and that we believe that there are certain conditions and circumstances that could reasonably be described as *causing* them to occur, in the self-same moment we are making it clear to people that they should not feel "let down," or disappointed by life, if a miracle does not occur in any particular case.

So the Divine Dichotomy there—the interesting circumstance—is that we invite people to use the power of positive thinking as part of a mental and spiritual approach to the creation of miracles, at the same time that we discourage people from expecting, demanding, or requiring that their spiritual approach will generate the outcomes that they desire.

DR. COOPER: I would venture to say that one of the *dangers* of spirituality today is the notion that there is a reliable "spiritual process" by which all illness can be cured. I do not believe this to be the case.

I believe it is a dangerous thought not only because it is untrue (or at least an "incomplete teaching"), but also because it causes people to feel *at fault* if they are unable to cure themselves. Some people may also go as far as to feel somehow metaphysically responsible for "attracting" the disease to themselves in the first place! So if we're not careful, this type of thinking can actually *multiply the negative effects of the disease.* There is a fine balance that needs to be respected here, and as a physician—as someone in the healing profession—I am acutely aware of it.

I would say that it impacts my work in two regards. First of all, it makes me very aware and cognizant of the effects it might have on a patient to give a specific *prognosis.* By prognosis, I mean an "expected outcome"—an expected trajectory for the disease, if you will.

While this information can be useful to patients, it can also be harmful to the degree that it closes one's mind to other possibilities. So in giving prognostic information to patients, I would assess each case separately in terms of how much information is helpful, and necessary, to share. Of course, if the patient specifically asked for it, it would be my professional duty to provide that information. However, if in doubt, I would allow more "room for error," so to speak . . . and more room for the soul to be invited in and to play a role in the patient's healing.

The second way it would impact my work is that it would change my definitions of "success" and "failure." So often in medicine these terms equate to "life" or "death," and "cure" or "no cure." In the medical profession, the urge to preserve life is so strong that we may be tempted to *see anything and everything else as a "failure."*

Yet how interesting it would be if doctors began to treat not just on the basis of *outcome*, but on the basis of *experience.* That is, if we could measure our "success" or "failure" as a physician not simply based on the patient's outcome—which is presumably their living or dying—but if we could consider our success based on our ability to facilitate the patient *having a better experience of their illness—including being okay with whatever's going on.*

Including coming to a place of total acceptance around whatever may be occurring with their health, *given that nothing can occur in our lives that does not serve a greater purpose at some level.*

So the over-arching point I am trying to make here is that perhaps the miracle doesn't simply have to be an outcome that is so remarkable that it defies medical knowledge. Perhaps it can simply be walking the road with the patient, and helping them to come to terms with their experience of the illness to the point where they *fully accept it.*

This, first of all, opens them to the *possibility* of a miracle, because from that place of acceptance we open ourselves to being able to create alternative outcomes, and secondly . . .

NEALE: That's precisely correct! *Because what you resist persists.*

DR. COOPER: And secondly, regardless of whether the "desired out-come" (life or death, cure or no cure) is achieved, *who's to say that any one outcome is "better," at the level of the soul?*

So perhaps the miracle is simply being okay with what is occurring. Because in being okay with what is occurring, rather than resisting it, you align yourself at all levels of creation.

You will therefore inevitably experience what is in your highest good.

NEALE: Yes, in my understanding that's precisely right.

DR. COOPER: Also, when I said earlier that I believe anyone who's soul absolutely and unequivocally desires a certain outcome will experience that outcome, *that statement comes with an important caveat.* And this is that we are not always consciously aware of the highest desires of our soul. In fact, very few people are, on a consistent basis. So to presume that we know what outcome is "best" is, in many cases, inaccurate.

"Healing," in my view, is not necessarily the "best outcome" as defined from a strictly medical point of view. I do not consider it to be the guarantee that whatever disease process is underway will be reversed, or "cured."

I believe that there are times when an illness is used as a means, or a vehicle, through which to demonstrate Divinity. And I also believe that there are times when "healing" is simply moving on—to another lifetime, and to another phase of the soul's journey.

NEALE: So it seems to me the true miracle is *acceptance.* Because, just as you said, acceptance opens the door to non-resistance. And non-resistance, in turn, opens the door to the far finer energies—the finer, more delicate, nuanced energies—that could and would, if there were any possibility for it to happen, produce what we call a *medical miracle.*

Because a medical miracle is defined in energetic terms as a change—and often a subtle change—in the *energy signature* of a person surrounding a particular physical condition or circumstance. And that energy shift is extremely nuanced, in comparison to the energy signature of a person who is *resigned* to their impending death or, even if it's not a terminal illness, to their particular condition. So I think there's a difference between being *accepting* and being *resigned.* And that's a difference we should be exploring verbally in this chapter.

A person who is *resigned* to their circumstance, whether it's . . . (feigned cough attack) . . . whether it's choking to death on the telephone, or some other circumstance—whether it's a non-terminal condition such as paralysis, or some handicap, or some debilitating circumstance that's not lethal, that's not life-threatening, but tremendously inconvenient, such as random nerve firings, we want to make a point in this chapter. We want to say to people: "Do not confuse being *resigned* to a circumstance with being *accepting* of a circumstance."

DR. COOPER: Absolutely.

NEALE: Because being *resigned* is a form of negative energy. The nuances of the energies are very delicate here, and the nuance of resignation is primarily negative. It doesn't have to, but it tends to mentally move toward closing off better possibilities.

"Oh well, I guess that's just the way it is, and I guess I don't have any choice. And so I best just be, you know, resigned to it and not fight it." That's a form of non-resistance, or non-opposition, but it's a negative form of non-opposition, as opposed to a positive form of non-opposition.

Acceptance, on the other hand, is the open acknowledgement that what is occurring is perfect and, unlike resignation, *it does not tend to close off future possibilities of any kind.*

DR. COOPER: What comes to mind as you say that, Neale, is that *resignation* seems to imply a subtle sense of *suffering* around whatever it is that one may be resigned about. Versus acceptance, which seems to offer a sense of *peace*, and from that sense of peace—I just have to insert this one thing—it has been shown in studies on meditation that a sense of peacefulness around something can actually create *biological changes at the cellular level, which promote healing!*[3]

So that nuance between *states of being*—between resignation and acceptance—actually produces *measurable biological changes* that can strengthen one's immune system, diminish inflammation, and demonstrably increase one's overall chance of a cure.

I just had to insert that little piece . . .

NEALE: That's good stuff. And now people can see the difference, just as there's a difference between the other side of resignation, where acceptance becomes—how would I call it—kind of a "Pollyanna" idea that *there's no doubt that total healing will occur.* Which is not what we're after, either.

But I'm wondering *where doubt comes in* . . . because that's a key question, metaphysically speaking.

DR. COOPER: It is.

NEALE: So we need to clarify in this chapter as well that to not doubt that a physical condition will be reversed (even a condition that would not require a "miracle" to occur for it to be reversed) opens one, as we said earlier, to the possibility of deep disappointment, anger with God, and horrific frustration that will only add to the negative medical condition. So not doubting that a reversal of even a minor medical condition will occur is not, I think, a healthy thing to advise or suggest.

Not doubting that the "perfect healing" will occur is another matter altogether. We then move to the point in this chapter where we have to define what we mean by "healing." Again, we spoke of this when we addressed the subject of miracles a moment ago.

Does healing equal the complete transformation and change of a medical condition, the shifting of a condition from one state to another, or does healing define a different transformation altogether? Could "healing" refer to a spiritual and mental transformation which may not produce any shift in the physical presenting of a circumstance, but may shift one's *mental and emotional experience* of it such that whatever was intended to be "healed" has been healed, in that we have stopped emotionally suffering from it?

DR. COOPER: I have two thoughts on that. I love these questions you're bringing up.

With regard to *doubt,* perhaps what we're seeking to no longer doubt is not what outcome specifically will occur, but to not doubt that whatever happens . . . how can I put this . . . I think that if we can come to the knowing that whatever happens will be . . .

NEALE: . . . to our highest benefit.

DR. COOPER: Yes!

You know, if my patients could know one thing, I would want them to know that *we're not going to go backwards in terms of our ability to express Divinity or to enjoy life* (when we consider life to be the eternal process of life). In other words, we're not going to be "worse off" spiritually because of a given medical outcome.

So I think the point we're trying to make here is to not doubt the outcome, regardless of what it is. Because whatever is occurring is *undoubtedly* (laughs), if I could use that word, yet another opportunity to continue to demonstrate higher and higher versions of ourselves.

Conversations with God points out that the purpose of life is to continually evolve into grander and grander versions of ourselves, and this process is not going to be reversed or made impossible by a so-called "negative outcome" with regards to our physical health. It is important to get very clear on this, *for it is the pathway to peace.*

NEALE: Indeed, there is no such thing as a negative outcome. And spiritual awareness provides that insight.

DR. COOPER: Exactly. Secondly, in regards to *healing,* my thoughts around healing have evolved so much since I first started medical school—this was before I knew you, Neale, and I thought that healing meant "curing the physical ailment." As you know, I'm very clear from our discussion today that this is a superficial and incomplete definition of healing.

Then about two or three years into my work towards my medical degree, I remember coming to the realization that healing involved more than the physical ailment, and that there was most certainly a mental and an emotional component to it as well. *But I've come even a step further than that now.*

To me, when I hear the word "healing" now, I hear something that reminds me of what your beautiful wife em said when she came downstairs to your family room to visit with us last week . . . and, hearing us talk about this book, she remarked: *"Maybe God and Medicine are One."*

So what I hear with the word "healing" now is: *Resolving the separation between the Journey of the Body and the Journey of the Soul.*

I'm not sure if that's the right way to put it . . .

NEALE: That's a great way to put it! *That's a great way to put it.*
    You raised my eyebrows when you said that. That is precisely correct. Nicely put.

DR. COOPER: Is that your thought on healing, too, then?

NEALE: Yes! I mean, I love what you just said!
    Healing is eliminating the difference . . . what did you just say? Eliminating the difference between . . .?

DR. COOPER: I said that healing is resolving the separation between the Journey of the Body and the Journey of the Soul. It is where the two become one.

It is, effectively, *where God and Medicine meet.* Which speaks to the title of this book.

NEALE: Yes. That is it! *That is it.* It re-words what we spoke of earlier, when we talked about the place where spirituality and physicality meet.
    Healing is when we see the two as one and, in fact, when we see all three—the physical, mental, and spiritual journeys—as part of a singular process. And seeing it in that way, it is impossible to hold that any particular aspect of it is somehow "out of alignment"—*such a thing would be impossible, given Who We Are.*

DR. COOPER: And when our body, mind, and soul are in alignment, all of our *levels of consciousness* are also in alignment.

Conversations with God talks about creating at the subconscious level, at the conscious level, at the superconscious level, and ultimately at the *supra*conscious level (all three combined). And when we're creating from the supraconscious level, I would venture to say that *everything is a miracle,* because we're creating exactly "on purpose," and exactly in alignment with the Agenda of our Soul.

NEALE: *With the greatest level of perfection.*

DR. COOPER: And with the greatest level of *efficiency* at doing so, because everything is in harmony.

NEALE: Yes. But the obvious question becomes, "How does one create outcomes in one's life?" That is more than I can go into in full here, because it's a whole book's worth of material, but the question is explored deeply in the book *Happier Than God*, which is part of the Conversations with God cosmology.

Briefly, creating at the supraconscious level involves setting aside all of one's own Little Me desires and opening to the vibrations of Absolute Needlessness and Unconditional Love that emanates from Divinity Itself. Those vibrations can be felt in every moment and at every Choicepoint in our lives. Responding to them becomes easier and easier the more we move deeply into the expression and experience of Who We Really Are, aided by an absolute determination and commitment with the Self to do so.

When we do, it turns out there's no such thing as an "unmiracle," because we see that everything that is happening is miraculously perfect.

DR. COOPER: Yes, I guess you could say that.

NEALE: *There's no such thing as an "unmiracle."*

Which is the reverse of "everything is a miracle."

There's no such thing as an unmiracle!

And when we believe that, and hold that to be true, we find and create enormous, enormous peace in our lives. *And if peace isn't the best medicine of all, then I don't know what is.*

If anything is going to have a medicinally healing effect—if anything is going to have an energetically beneficial effect on our lives at any level—it is going to be the energy that we call, in human language, *peace.* Which is the quietest form of Love.

Peace is the quietest form of Love.

DR. COOPER: And peace is, at the very least, *the absence of suffering.* Which I think is what we're truly trying to avoid. I don't think we're trying to avoid death nearly so much as we're trying to avoid suffering . . .

NEALE: I agree.

DR. COOPER: Suffering around the uncertainty of death, or around the idea of intolerable pain. One of those. But I think suffering is the ultimate outcome we are trying to avoid.

NEALE: Yes.

DR. COOPER: And if you have peace, you don't have suffering. *So the struggle ends there.*

NEALE: Nice.

DR. COOPER: Shall we move onto the next topic now? I feel complete with this one.

NEALE: Onward, then.

Chapter Seven

THE MEDICAL SYSTEM:
Is There a Place for God?

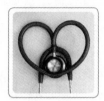

DR. COOPER: If healing is *the point at which the Journey of the Body and the Journey of the Soul become One,* it invites us to consider the role of physicians in an entirely new light. It brings up a whole new series of questions.

How, if at all, can physicians adopt this new viewpoint on healing? Is it possible to incorporate into the western medical model? If so, how would it change the way we show up in the room of patients?

There is just so much to consider here . . .

NEALE: There is. But first, let me say something. The sadness about the medical profession, from my point of view as a layperson, is that the whole of the medical intervention in a person's life seems to be directed at avoiding death in the patient. That a doctor considers himself to be "successful" if he's managed to keep the patient alive. And she imagines that she is a "failure" if she has not kept the patient alive.

Now I know we spoke of this earlier, and this relates to some of what we touched on in that earlier exchange. What I'm saying here is that medicine—modern medicine—tends to measure "success" or "failure" by a simple and rather crude measuring stick:

> Level 1: Did the patient survive or not?

> Level 2: Was the patient relieved of abject suffering, or was he not? And . . .

> Level 3: Did this patient's health, and did this patient's condition, improve or did it not?

Those seem to be the three levels of measurement, as I observed it, by which physicians determine whether they've been successful or not successful in their intervention with the patient.

Sadly, at none of those three levels *is the patient's spiritual well-being even considered or focused on.* Which is ironic, because their spiritual well-being could conceivably play an enormous role in the other three areas that are being measured by physicians!

But when physicians approach a patient, by and large (this seems to me to be true with the largest percentage of physicians in the world), they approach the patient and they measure the effectiveness of their interaction with the patient based on those three criteria. Did they survive? Was their suffering reduced? And ultimately, has their health actually improved?

At no point is there a measurement of *what their spiritual experience has been.* Which brings up the question of *how doctors are being educated in the field of spirituality*—and what role, if any, the physician has in igniting, arousing, and impacting or affecting the spiritual response mechanism of the patient.

There are certain healing mechanisms of all patients—the immune system being the obvious one, and there are others as well—that physicians are trained to trigger. They can either trigger it pharmaceutically, or they can trigger it mechanically through a thing called surgery, or they can trigger it psychologically, as you said earlier, by the way they walk into the room and the way they talk. But how does the physician trigger the patient's *spiritual* healing mechanisms? *Or, does the physician even have a role in doing that?*

I would argue that she does, but the medical profession over the past several hundred years appears to have paid scarce attention to that, *and, I think, to its failing.*

DR. COOPER: I agree! *Conversations with God* makes it clear that we are three-part beings, composed of Body, Mind, and Soul. Medicine focuses primarily on the physical, and it is at best a blend of the physical and the mental/emotional aspects of healing (for those doctors who are kind enough to have what we would call "good bedside manner"). However, rarely, if ever, is the soul brought in. So it's like riding a tricycle with only one or two wheels and wondering why, even after we've "fixed it," it's still broken!

And I believe it's because we have failed to address the full picture—and we have missed out on what is arguably the most important aspect of Who We Are. And this is the connection to our soul, to our Highest Self, and to the real reason we are here on the planet.

When we begin to embrace a more "holistic viewpoint," one that honors the Body-Mind-Soul Triad, *it changes everything*—from our experience of the illness to our experience of the very thing we call "healing." In my opinion, being "healed" and being "cured of a physical ailment" are not the same thing, as we have now discussed several times. And the mere fact that a patient "survived" does not by any means guarantee a life filled with joy and peace, free of suffering.

A life filled with joy and peace, free of suffering, *is a spiritual choice.* It has little to do with the circumstances of our lives, and much to do with how we choose to *relate* to those circumstances.

This is powerfully illustrated by the late Ken Keyes Jr., author of *Handbook to Higher Consciousness.*[7] Keyes experienced the great "tragedy" of becoming a quadriplegic (paralyzed from the neck down) at the young age of 25, secondary to contracting polio. Yet rather than allowing this unexpected and perhaps unfortunate turn of events to be his downfall, he used it as a platform from which to experience his Highest Self.

He moved into a place of *acceptance*, and ultimately into a space of *gratitude,* for the adversity with which he was faced, and he learned to free himself from mental and spiritual suffering, despite the limitations placed upon his physical body. Ken Keyes Jr. went on to become a great teacher and mentor to others, for he illustrated what it truly means to be "healed"—not strictly in the physical sense, but in the more global sense of knowing and experiencing Who We Really Are and why we're on the planet.

This inevitably leads us to ask: *could Ken Keyes Jr. have achieved such a profound and inspiring transformation in his life without having contracted polio? In this context, was his illness a setback or a springboard?*

For that matter, the way we see *anything* in our lives—as a *challenge* or as an *opportunity*—is entirely our choice, and this is precisely the point that the life of Ken Keyes Jr. illustrates.

Indeed, it is where the spiritual part of healing comes in.

NEALE: Ken explored this question in a book that he authored about this period in his life, titled *Discovering The Secrets of Happiness*. In it Ken himself suggested that his disability may have been a blessing in disguise. He wrote:

"Perhaps I would have been so caught up in the business and social rat race that I wouldn't have sat still long enough to study my security, sensation and power illusions — and then discover how to deal with them so I could open up my heart to loving more. My reality is that I am far too busy and involved in my life activities to have time to concern myself with self-consciousness in the wheelchair department. Today I view my so-called 'handicap' as another gift my life has offered me."

The reason Ken Keyes' book *Handbook to Higher Consciousness* is so powerful, the reason it sold so many copies and touched so many people, is that his personal life setback was so dramatic. People could not help but look at his situation and think, "Oh, my gosh! If you can reframe your point of view around being paralyzed from the neck down, if you can still see your life and your situation as a *blessing*, then for heaven's sake, who am I to complain?!"

I had the privilege of meeting Ken Keyes in person shortly after *Conversations with God* was published.

DR. COOPER: He sounds like a truly remarkable and deeply inspiring man.

NEALE: He was. He most certainly was. He has since celebrated his Continuation Day.

DR. COOPER: I know you have mentioned him in a number of your *Conversations with God* books. It is no small feat to live an entire life wheelchair-bound, paralyzed from the neck down, and to still powerfully believe that you have *everything you need within you to live a life of complete happiness and fulfillment*. We certainly don't witness many people living that kind of a life.

This is why Keyes is a perfect illustration of the larger point we are trying to make here . . . which is that true healing cannot occur unless and until we have addressed the larger metaphysical picture of what is going on with the patient spiritually.

NEALE: So the question then becomes: Does the medical profession, as a field, even begin to consider the validity of what you've just said at any level? Is there any room in the current operating model *for a metaphysical aspect?*

DR. COOPER: I would say, as far as my experience has been, the answer is no. I would say that we are shifting toward more of a holistic, all-encompassing, and perhaps even verging on a "mental-emotional-spiritual" approach to health and well-being . . . but that it is not even close to being at the level of which you are speaking. It is getting closer, but it is certainly not "there" yet, which is why I think having conversations like this one, about what it might look like, are an important first step.

With that said, there are certainly doctors who "break the traditional mold," and who are taking the first steps and paving the way for others to follow. And these doctors have been a huge inspiration to me in my own journey. *But it has been their own choice to bring that metaphysical aspect, or spiritual energy, into the room.* It hasn't been based on their medical training, as far as I know.

There is one story that is particularly touching that I would like to share here.

This particular case was a baby who was born prematurely at 23-and-a-half weeks—just a few days before what is called the "threshold of viability" (which is the minimum age for a baby to survive, and is normally at 24 weeks). Anytime before that their little bodies are just not ready to survive in the outside world. Their lungs, for instance, will not be sufficiently developed to breathe, and their digestive tracts will not be developed enough to absorb their mother's breast milk. They are close to being able to survive, but not quite there.

The little baby boy I am talking about here was just a few days shy of the developmental stage he needed to attain in order to survive in the outside world. His mother was overwhelmed with worry, sadness and grief as the doctors regrettably told her that her baby would in all likelihood not survive. He was simply too young. In fact, the odds were a hundred to one that he wasn't going to make it. It would have been nothing short of a miracle should this young baby boy have successfully made the transition from the womb to the outside world.

But here's what shocked me. Here's what touched me. *And here is the piece that I will never ever forget, for as long as I live and for as long as I practice medicine.*

And this is that, despite the seemingly tragic and hopeless nature of the situation, the two medical specialists—the Neonatologist and the Obstetrician—offered to be present for the birth. Even though the chances of the baby surviving were next to nil, they offered their presence as an emotional support to the mother and to the family, if nothing else. They said to the mother, "We are here in the tiny chance that something can be done to help your baby . . . and if not, we are here for *you*."

Sure enough, the baby did not survive. Out he came, the smallest thing I had ever seen, not more than eight inches long with legs and arms as thin as a dime. The specialists examined him briefly, but they knew he would not live more than a few minutes. They gently handed him to his mother, where she shared a precious moment with him before he quietly passed in her arms.

However, the remarkable thing is that, despite the *outcome* (which many would consider to be negative, and certainly a "failure" by any medical standard), the *healing* that took place in that room was both breathtaking and transformative. It was unlike anything I had ever seen in my life!

These specialists are the only two doctors I have seen let down their walls and cry with a patient. They shared in the sadness of the moment and, although they did nothing to change the *outcome,* simply their presence and their way of being was *healing.* I know it was healing! For it created an environment for that mother and for that family where, despite the tragic nature of what occurred, they felt like they were not alone. And they felt like their *experience* was, I think to some degree, healed . . . or at least faster on the road to being healed.

However, I have never seen this sort of "holistic approach" to healing included in our medical training. I have observed it from time to time—and I have huge admiration for those physicians who take their work to that *metaphysical level*—but I would absolutely say that it is something they do of their own accord.

NEALE: Do you think there's a place for it, or do you think that there *should be*—I should restate that question—do you think there *should be,* and would you recommend that there absolutely be, a place in modern medical training, in preparing a person to be a physician, *for metaphysical knowledge and practices?*

DR. COOPER: Personally, I absolutely think that there should be a place for it in the medical profession and in medical school training. And I can't even count the number of patients who would agree with me!

I say that because so many people have been dissatisfied with their experience in the healthcare system—and, perhaps surprisingly, the largest number of "complaints" are not about the medical treatments themselves, but rather about the lack of mental, emotional, and spiritual care that accompanies them. I could be wrong about this, but it has certainly been my observation.

So yes, in answer to your question, I absolutely think there is a place for what we could loosely call *spirituality* in modern medical schools. And there are a few reasons I think this.

First of all, the current medical model is based much more on *quantity of life* rather than *quality of life*. But I think what people are really interested in—what's at the heart of the matter, so to speak—is healing their *quality of life*. In other words, *of having an experience here on the planet that is truly fulfilling*. Which makes perfect sense when you think about it. I mean, the whole reason that people are showing up at your retreats is because their experience of life is not fulfilling, *whether they have a medical condition or not*.

And so I think every single profession, medicine included, should prioritize bringing forth that spiritual and metaphysical aspect, which taps us back into the real reason we're here. *What's the point of staying alive, of preserving life, if we're not going to do it in a way that is fulfilling?* I think all too many patients are discharged from the hospital in a state that is so-called "cured," but is really lacking in the patient's own fulfillment. *I would be hard-pressed to call that a "cure" when it comes to the real reason that we're here on Earth.*

NEALE: But the challenge in the medical profession is that if we bring metaphysics into the physics of medicine, we are stymied, because the question becomes: which metaphysical model, which belief system, which spiritual thought system, should prevail, should be taught, in a medical school?

Do we declare that a thing that's called God exists? Or, do we use a reductionist approach and simply say, "Let's not call it God, but let's all acknowledge at least from a scientific point of view that there's such a thing as energy in the Universe . . . that All of Life is made up of energy, and that this energy can be manipulated and focused with predictable and consistent results?"

If we believe that, should we have a course in medical school that teaches how we can focus this universal energy that we call Life with predictable and consistent results? Should we have courses in our medical schools about how those results can be created and tabulated and measured and turned into some equally predictable outcome, as we do with how we measure other outcomes in the medical field?

This raises just a bazillion interesting questions about how you would insert metaphysics into medical training, *and the inability to answer those questions is no doubt why it hasn't become part of medical training.*

So ironically enough, members of one of the most critical and crucial occupations on the Earth—the occupation of those who keep us alive, and those who heal our most challenging physical conditions—are not receiving any training whatsoever in the one area of human expression that could be the most powerful single area affecting their physical and mental condition.

DR. COOPER: *It is ironic.* Gosh, when you put it that way—but yes, it makes total sense, for it would indeed create incessant controversy as to which religion or spirituality to pick, which God to honor, and how (if at all) to incorporate the soul into the practice of medicine.

This would make it exceedingly difficult, if not impossible, for people to come up with a curriculum, or a "gold standard" of practice, upon which everyone could agree. So it is completely understandable why the medical profession, to date, has avoided and in fact discouraged any overlap with spirituality or religion of any kind.

Yet I do not think the situation is hopeless.

To the contrary, I feel very *hopeful* that we could, in fact, include God in the medical school curriculum. And I would suggest it is simpler than we might think, and that we do not have to "choose one way to do it." I think there could in fact be many ways, tailored to each individual person and to each particular setting. And we could create a set of *principles* rather than requirements, to allow people the freedom to bring God forth *in whatever way best serves the moment and the people involved.*

You know, Neale, a thought just came to my mind. It would be wonderful if we could just encourage among physicians the willingness to ask the Four Fundamental Questions of Life . . . those questions we touched upon at the very start of this book: Who am I? Where am I? Why am I where I am? What do I intend to do about that?

Which is, essentially, to ask ourselves, *why am I in the space?*

I will never forget when I was telling you about my struggles as a medical student, and you stopped me in my tracks to gently say: *Brit, consider the reason you're in the space.* And even if we just encouraged everyone to answer that question for themselves, I think it would make a world of difference. I mean, imagine if every single doctor reflected for a moment or two before walking into the patient's room, and really asked themselves, "What am I doing here? Am I getting though as many patients as I can as fast as I can to get the highest paycheck in the least amount of time? Perhaps. Or, is it possible that I am here to serve a spiritual agenda, both for myself in terms of how I show up, as well as for my patient? If so, *how might that look?*"

I vividly remember when you asked me that question. I was totally caught off guard. Never before had I heard anyone consider a medical encounter from that point of view. *And it changed my whole reason for going into the room!* I thought, "Yeah, you know what, I *am* here to serve a spiritual agenda." And whatever I happened to decide in that moment was my "agenda," it almost didn't matter, for it was more about *the elevated consciousness, and the heightened state of being, that surrounded that decision.*

I became very clear that my reason for showing up in the room involved a *metaphysical aspect*, and that simple acknowledgement changed everything.

NEALE: I'm here for a reason that transcends the physicality of the moment.

I am here for a reason that transcends the physicality of the moment!

DR. COOPER: I like that sentence!

NEALE: Yes, and it drives directly to the question, *What is the purpose of Life itself?* And what is the purpose of *this moment,* interior to that larger agenda?

Chapter Eight

A LOOK TO OUR FUTURE:
Healing Humanity's Experience of Itself

DR. COOPER: I think it is time we take a look at our future—and not only the future of medical science but, perhaps most importantly, the future of humanity.

I would like to start by talking about some new and exciting medical technology, the advent of which causes us to question things not just medically, but *spiritually.*

Do you remember the Human Genome Project that got so much attention back in 2003? It was the world's first "blueprint" of the human genome, allowing us a never-before-seen glimpse into the way in which Nature has created our species. It was such a revolutionary discovery that it was compared to when man first landed on the moon!

Anyway, I recently took a course that focused largely on the up-and-coming directions of medical practice, and one of the highlights was this business of "genetic medicine" that I would love to touch on with you here today. And it goes well beyond the Human Genome Project into the realm of *personalized genetic sequencing* as a foreseeable standard of everyday medical care.

Believe it or not, in the next fifty years, it is projected that every single patient will have their entire genome sequenced and on record in their family doctor's office. This will provide all sorts of information that will allow us, as doctors, to personally tailor medical treatments and diagnoses in ways we never previously imagined possible.

Medicine used to be based on a "one-size-fits-all" kind of model. A patient would present with symptoms, and we would prescribe an investigation plan, a treatment plan, and so on and so forth on the assumption that this was most efficient and effective method to return people to good physical health. But it turns out this "one-size-fits-all" model really isn't the most effective way of doing things after all. And this is because everyone is unique, and everyone responds differently. *And much of this can be predicted by a person's genes.*

For example, there was a recent feature piece in the Globe and Mail newspaper talking about genetic treatments for cystic fibrosis.[8] The article described a new drug called Kalydeco, which, for the select 4 percent of the cystic fibrosis population with a certain genetic muta-tion (there are different genetic variants of the disease), *could change their whole life in an instant.*

Normally, when a child is diagnosed with cystic fibrosis, their qual-ity of life is greatly diminished. However, if they have this particular genetic variant and receive the drug, their entire life can be turned around! *So it is a powerful example of how individualized treatment can save a life.*

The caveat of what some call the "miracle drug" for cystic fibrosis, though, is that it costs $300,000 per year for one patient in Canada. But cost relates to the novelty of a treatment, and soon genetic-based treatments are expected to be the norm and accessible to everyone.

Another example of the use of personalized genetic medicine—this time in the area of cancer prevention—is Angelina Jolie's story. Magazines were covered with the news when Jolie decided to get a double mastectomy (both breasts prophylactically removed) because her mother had been diagnosed with breast cancer and Jolie had also been found to have the BRCA1 gene. This meant that, based on her genetics, Angelina Jolie had an 87 percent chance of developing breast cancer, and a 50 percent chance of developing ovarian cancer.[9]

According to *Huffington Post* reporters, the amount of women seeking breast cancer genetic screening has increased by 90 percent since Jolie went public about her procedure.[5] It certainly shows how genetic information, and a "personalized approach" to medicine, can have huge advantages, both preventatively as well as treatment-wise. And as it becomes more and more of a societal norm, it will have greater and greater impacts on people.

NEALE: Think of all the things that will be happening in your life and in your career . . . that *are* happening, I should say. That is remarkable.

DR. COOPER: It totally is. But there is a reason I brought that up. *A reason that goes far beyond the medical.*

My larger, over-arching observation is that what we have done in medicine—in terms of creating a focus toward "individualized" treatment plans and getting rid of the "one-size-fits-all" model—we have done in many other areas of life as well. We have done it in technology, developing personalized features on our cell phones, laptops, and tablets. We have done it in real estate, personalizing our preferences in homes, locations, furniture and décor. We have done it in education, tailoring our courses and our interests to our unique personalities, goals, and desires.

But the one area it seems to me we have utterly failed to do this is in our spirituality. Which may just be the most crucial area of all!

So my question becomes: What would it take for our culture to encourage a personal relationship with God? In other words, what would it take to promote unique and individual expressions of the Divinity within each of us?

Spirituality seems to me to be the one area with the most pressure to conform. This expectation exists so strongly and so powerfully that to even propose the idea of having a "conversation with God," as you did Neale, would likely be considered totally absurd and even blasphemous. *Yet it is clear to anyone who has read even one of your books how dramatically and beautifully that experience changed your life.*

Quite simply, our unique spiritual expression is the reason we have come to the planet. Yet it is the area that receives the least attention and the least validation; that is, our Cultural Story encourages everything *except* a personal, *two-way* relationship with God.

Surely, if we can devote all of that time and money to personally sequencing each person's genome, we can devote even a fraction of that to encouraging each person to engage with and to connect with their Highest Self spiritually. *Or, is that asking too much?*

NEALE: The reason that very, very few people find themselves motivated, inspired, or encouraged to develop an individuated experience of their spirituality—a personalized two-way experience of God—is that they have been encouraged not to, just as you pointed out. But it's even greater than that.

Most people are not even *aware* that life is *primarily a spiritual experience;* that the purpose of life in the physical has to do with the spiritual experience of each human soul.

So the real larger reason that people don't find themselves motivated to create a personal two-way experience of God is that they are not even clear that the purpose of life has very little to do with their purely physical expressions. I wrote in *The Only Thing That Matters* that 98 percent of the world's people are spending 98 percent of their time on things that don't matter.

So I am shockingly observant of the fact that the largest number of people *by far*—not 60 or 70 percent, but 85 or 90 percent of the world's people—are simply engaged in day-to-day life, week-to-week creations, month-to-month manifestations, and year-to-year goal-setting of what they're trying to produce in their life. They are striving and yearning and searching for what it is they imagine they would like to experience in order to be "successful" and happy. And the number of people, on a percentage basis, that understand that the *whole purpose of life on Earth is to move forward the Agenda of the Soul* is astonishingly low. Given this, people would not be motivated to create a personal experience of God.

The interesting thing about what you're bringing up is that, as we increase our ability to keep people physically well, and maybe extend their life expectancy—perhaps beyond what anyone in this moment could even begin to imagine—the interesting thing about that is this: Unless we lay the groundwork in the minds of human beings that allows them to know that this creates an *even larger platform*, an *even more wondrous stage*, upon which they can build the outcomes that produce the experiences *for which their soul yearns*—unless we cause them to see that—the longer lifespan and the greater health maintenance that we can produce with these modern medical miracles will, if we're not careful, actually work against our whole reason for staying alive.

So the irony is that the reason for staying alive could very well be defeated by the fact that we are creating ways for us to stay alive longer and longer and longer. And that's only true in the culture of our particular species. That is, Earthlings, people, human beings. Because we are a very, very young species.

The older, more mature species of sentient beings in the universe are very well aware that their ability to visibly physicalize and interact with each other and with the rest of the physical environment that we call the known universe is the greatest gift, *precisely because it gives them an unparalleled opportunity to complete the Agenda of their Spiritual Selves*—which can only be completed in the Realm of the Physical. Or, if you please, in the Realm of the Relative.

And so, the sentient beings elsewhere in the universe, many species of which are far more mature than we are, are clear about the *golden treasure that is theirs*. And they are living, of course, way, way, way beyond anything we could imagine.

For instance, *Conversations with God* made the interesting point in its dialogue *that we were meant to live forever;* that physical life was designed to allow sentient beings to live essentially forever. *And not to have to die at all,* unless they actively chose to, perhaps after several hundred years in one particular bodily expression, at which point they could choose to recreate themselves anew in a different expression, for a wide variety of reasons, but having nothing to do with typical end-of-life reasons that are faced routinely now by human beings on the Earth.

So the fact is that we are dying at a ridiculously young age of anywhere between 60 and 90, for the most part. We are leaving our physical body at a very young age if you count those who won't even make it that long, if you count those who get into an accident or something, or have some illness at a very young age. But a sign of the exponential increase in the maturity of our species is exactly what you're pointing to.

We are, indeed, learning how to extend the lifespan and increase the good health of human beings, such that the instructors in your school are absolutely correct: In the next fifty years we could very well have achieved the potential to live far past the age of 100. *That might one day even seem like middle age to us.*

Soon *biogenetic medicine* is going to give us the opportunity to actually replace and recreate whole organs in the body. So there will be very little reason, in fifty or sixty years, for us to have to die. And we won't be dying of "old age," that's for sure. Because we'll be able to replace all of our old parts, our "aging parts," with brand new parts. And so "old age" will no longer be a reason to expire. We still might have accidents—that's of course true—and we may be so injured that we can't put Humpty Dumpty back together again. But "old age" may be a virtually unheard of reason for us to leave physical form.

That is going to create a tremendous conundrum for people. Because then they'll have to *really* start asking themselves the kinds of questions we ask ourselves now, when we get as old as I am. Then the human species will really have to start to ask itself, you know, "What is the point? What am I doing here for 120, 150, 170 years, or more?

"*What actually is the point of this physical platform that I have found myself on?*"

And surely it will be very clear when we start living to be 120, 140, or 150 years old that it obviously can't be about get the guy, get the girl, get the car, get the job . . . *There clearly is something else going on.* And that will become patently obvious to us, as we begin living so long that we become bored with nothing but the physical accouterments of our life.

So the extended lifespan of humanity is going to create a real conundrum for human beings. And the question is: Will it work *against* the Agenda of the Soul, or *in favor of* the Agenda of the Soul?

And that question will be placed before the house, and answered by people who are paying particular and specific attention to not only the health of the body, but to the existence of the human soul and its purpose and function in the overall process that we call human life.

DR. COOPER: Yes! It certainly will bring up that important question: are we here to serve the *Agenda of the Body* (to gather the physical accouterments of life, as you put it), or are we in fact here to serve the *Agenda of the Soul?* And it would certainly change our experience dramatically, in particular our *spiritual experience,* if we were to live for 150 years!

I notice coming to your retreats that often people will hit that point of spiritual inquiry around mid-life with our current lifespan. Because, as you said, the whole "to-do list" of get the guy, get the girl, get the car, get the house etc., is no longer a novelty. And people come to see, maybe around forty, fifty, or sixty: *Okay, I've done that, and that was wonderful . . . but maybe now there's something more!*

So perhaps that would all be even more magnified with a lifespan two times as long!

NEALE: Imagine that! Imagine if you'd gotten done all the things you thought you were supposed to get done by the age of 45, or 50, or even 60. *Now what are you going to do for the next hundred years?!!*

DR. COOPER: (Laughs.) That's a really good question.

NEALE: *That's the question that medical science had better be prepared to answer.*

Because doctors are going to become more than just healers and "life extenders"—they're going to become *life explainers.* People are going to be going to doctors saying, "Whoa," you know, *"What do I do now for the next hundred years?* I already got the guy, got the girl, got the car, got the job . . . *now what am I going to do?"*

And we're going to find that the doctors who call themselves psychiatrists, who are, of course, medical doctors, are going to have enormously different kinds of work to do. In fact, there will be a *brand new field*, as physicians in other fields begin to extend the lifespan of human beings. Doctors of the mind—psychiatrists (I promise you, and I predict that this will happen in your lifetime)—will develop a new occupation, a new branch and a new field of Psychiatry. It'll be called . . . I don't know what they'll call it ultimately, but my description of it would be *Spiritual Psychiatry.*

My understanding is that the word "psychology" is a derivative of two words, "psycho" and "logy," which emerge from the Greek word for *soul*, and the Greek word for *logic*, or *wisdom*. So "psycho-logy" is the wisdom or the logic of the soul.

They took the soul out of "psycho-logy" when it became "psychology" (the profession), and these days psychologists and psychiatrists are not allowed to bring into their treatment the word God, unless it is at the behest and at the specific request of the patient. But even then, they can only ask the patient what they think about that. It is considered out of bounds for psychiatrists to propose or suggest or explore ideas about God that the psychiatrist puts into the space. They can only discuss what the patient brings into the conversation.

But there will be Spiritual Therapists as a branch of Psychiatry and Psychology in the next fifty years who will be just as much a specialist in that area as eye, ear, nose, and throat specialists, and other physicians who specialize in certain areas of the physical body, are today. The *metaphysical* discipline will join the *physical* disciplines as part of the overall medical profession.

DR. COOPER: That's such a beautiful way of putting it—the *meta-physical* will join the *physical.*

This whole concept makes me think back to a doctor I worked with who was a Pediatric Oncologist, meaning that she worked in the field of *childhood cancer.* Many people would consider this to be a challenging if not a deeply saddening field to work in, given that many of these children never make it into their adult years. But what this doctor offered these children is a gift I'll never forget. She was certainly a "Doctor of the Soul," if I could put it that way . . . someone who merged the *physical* with the *metaphysical,* to use your words.

As we've talked about before, in the chapter on medical miracles, healing the *physical* and the *metaphysical* are *two sides of the same coin.* It is in the Intersection of the Physical and the Spiritual—where God and Medicine meet—where true healing takes place. For in situations as dramatic and life-changing as childhood cancer, *to heal the body without taking into account the spiritual journey of the individual would be to consider just one small piece of the pie.*

And this is what separated this particular physician from anyone else I've worked with. She took children, many of whom were in a "tragic situation" when we consider life from a purely physical point of view, *and she understood at an intuitive level how to nurture these children's souls.*

I remember being so touched, Neale, by the way she walked through the world. Every week, she would get the kids together and volunteer her time for a "group outing." Sometimes it would be an outdoor activity like going for a walk in the woods, or having a picnic, and other times it would be an indoor activity like arts and crafts or watching a movie with pizza. All of the kids would get together with one another, *but the rule was that they could not talk about cancer.* Each one of them had cancer, and each one of them had been enduring challenging health battles, but for the duration of the evening they got to experience being normal, regular children, free from the psychological burdens of chronic disease.

All they were to do was to "hang out" with one another, to spend quality time, and to celebrate their gifts. So every activity they would do—whether it was arts and crafts, whether it was walking in nature, no matter what it was—this doctor would point out to them their talents and their successes. *And she would celebrate the gifts that they each had in this lifetime.* And whether your life is 7 years or 17 years or 70 years long, to me in that moment I felt like gosh, *it almost doesn't make a difference.*

Because what she was teaching these children was to live a spiritual life in the time they were here. And rather than feeling like their life was "worse off," these kids were actually some of the happiest children I'd ever met! Every time they saw this particular doctor, they walked into the room with a smile on their face and with joy pouring out of their hearts. And I think it's because, although these kids had a fraction of time on the planet compared with our current life expectancy, she was teaching them how to live in alignment with the *Agenda of the Soul.*

So while their bodies may have been "dying," their souls were not. And to that degree, their lives were . . .

NEALE: . . . complete.

DR. COOPER: Yes! Their lives were *complete.* And if this isn't true healing, *then I don't know what is.*

To me, it illustrates perfectly what we've been talking about in this conversation—and in the whole book, actually. *That the whole point of even having a physical life is as a vehicle to express what our soul desires to experience,* which can only be experienced in the Realm of the Relative, as you said several minutes ago.

And this story really illustrates to me how, regardless of the time we have in this particular lifetime—in this particular physical expression—there is always enough time to complete the Agenda of the Soul, *when we create the opportunity for our gifts to shine and to remember the real reason we're here.*

However, it is very true that if we were around for 120, 150, or 170 years, it would certainly be much harder *not* to contemplate the Agenda of the Soul, and *not* to consider the whole point for us being here on the planet. So having a longer lifespan would definitely pose the question in a more vivid, a more noticeable, and a more powerful way than it ever has been before.

NEALE: It would pose the question in a way that is essentially *unavoidable*.

DR. COOPER: Exactly. On the topic of expanded life spans, then, may we switch gears for just a moment?

NEALE: Sure. What is your question?

DR. COOPER: I am wondering about your thoughts on the idea of freezing a body in hopes of bringing it back years down the road? I know this sounds totally science fiction, but it is actually a real thing. And it is a remarkable procedure. The medical term for it is *cryonics,* or *cryopreservation.*[10]

What it entails is having your body or your brain "frozen" after you pass away, in hopes that you may be "unfrozen" and brought back to life years down the road (when medical science has caught up and "created a cure," so to speak, for whatever illness you passed away from).

I recently read an interview with Larry King talking about how he was hoping to be "cryopreserved," or frozen, after he died, so that he can hopefully come back one day.[11]

I'm curious what you think of this, Neale . . . and whether it's even necessary, or for that matter advisable, from a spiritual point of view . . .

NEALE: Well it's *unnecessary*, given the Agenda of the Soul, but it is not necessarily undesirable or somehow spiritually unworthy.

It's unnecessary in the sense that the soul can achieve what it wishes to achieve, what it seeks to achieve, through the multiplicity of lifetimes—the *endless* number of lifetimes—that the soul, throughout eternity, may experience. But if the mind is particularly attracted to and fond of a particular expression in physical form, there's no reason in the world why, if it can be done, that a person should or could not be brought back to physical life after such a procedure. And such an eventuality would certainly not inhibit in any way the continued and further evolution of the soul.

So it's no more deleterious, and no more damaging or obstructive to the overall process of evolution, than the opposite of that, which would be suicide, or the intentional ending of one's life.

Conversations with God has made it very clear to me that the intentioned ending of one's life is not a spiritual offense. It's not "held against" a soul (nothing, in fact, is), and it in no way inhibits or holds the soul back from its ability to continue to evolve, and to create and express larger and larger versions of itself. So if *ending* one's life is not considered at some level spiritually inappropriate, or non-beneficial, then certainly *extending* one's life—by whatever means, including being brought back after being frozen—likewise would not be spiritually inappropriate or *ipso facto* non-beneficial.

I think what would happen, though—my prediction would be— that I would eventually become so complete with being Neale, as Larry might eventually become so complete with being Larry King, that he would willingly . . . and this is the irony of it . . . I suspect that, should the miracle actually come to pass that people can have their bodies frozen and then brought back to life when medical science catches up to what caused their death and reverse the process, the irony is that a large number of those people would then, I suspect, eventually choose euthanasia—the deliberate *ending* of their life!

And there's the irony of it.

And I mean ultimately. Not as soon as they woke up and got unfrozen. They'd say, "Oh wow! It worked! Here I am!" But after a while, the irony is that the very people who jumped over great hurdles and contorted the whole experience such that they would freeze themselves in order to extend their lives, those very people might very well then ultimately voluntarily euthanize themselves. Because they would get to the point where they would say, "Oh, my gosh, you mean I'm going be Larry King for the rest of all eternity? *I don't think so.*"

Not because there's anything wrong with being Larry King, or Neale Donald Walsch, for all of eternity. *But we would run out of original or new ways to express in this particular form; ways that continued to stimulate and inspire the Self through the process.*

You know, if we think that marriages can sometimes go sour and go south and get boring after being married for fifty, sixty, or seventy years, imagine being married to *yourself* for 150 years!

DR. COOPER: (Laughs.) It's such a fascinating perspective that you have!

NEALE: Yes, so I think that what would happen is that the Larry Kings of the world would eventually become bored, out of their sense of Completion!

Okay, I've done all the things that I could do. And I've done it over and over again, and I think, you know, I want a new pair of shoes!

So for the same reason that we go into our closet and throw out the old things, even though a lot of them are still perfectly wearable—we send them to the second-hand store, or to Goodwill—because even though they are perfectly wearable, *we are tired of wearing them.* They haven't worn out, we're just tired of wearing them "out." So they stay in the closet for six years, having not been worn out in ages.

And we would feel the same way about our body. We haven't "worn it out," especially with this new process where we can be brought back to life after being frozen. However, we would then go into the "closet" of our mind and realize that, "Okay, this body hasn't worn out—it still can function—but I'm turning it in. *I'm turning it in.* Because I want a new body! I want a new physical experience, just like I want a new jacket. I've had this one for many years, and I'm done with it."

So I think that one of the great adventures for humanity is the "unexperienced" and the "not yet done." I think that's true, by the way, of all sentient beings. We strive for that which has not yet been done and that which has not yet been experienced.

I think that sentient beings are by nature explorers, expanding into the farthest reaches of their physical universe, and the farthest reaches of their metaphysical experience. Both! To, as Gene Roddenberry said, "Go where no man has gone before." And I think that we would be squashing that impulse if we had to continue going where we've gone before, over and over and over again, forever and ever and ever. And that would not feel very good to us.

Ultimately, the fundamental impulse and the fundamental instinct of life itself *is to renew itself in new forms.* And this would overtake the desire to remain in our old form. *And we would choose euthanasia* to resolve the dilemma.

DR. COOPER: I find this discussion so fascinating, because I agree with you that all human beings do have that fundamental instinct to change, to evolve, and to grow into grander and grander versions and expressions of the Self. And I agree we would not be satisfied for 150 years to repeat the same story, to repeat the same expressions, and we would intuitively—and at the soul level—seek that expansion.

Yet it's ironic, because at the same time—and I don't know if this is a matter of a feeling of *control* or what it is—it seems that when the outcome appears to be "out of our control," such as our death, we suddenly have the desire to cling desperately to what we have. *And it seems to me that this is what leads to the desire to be frozen and to come back.*

So perhaps it is more of an issue of feeling "in control." And when we can understand that our soul is *willingly choosing everything*, including the time and the place of our death, perhaps we can move forward into the next expression of ourselves with less resistance, and more joy.

NEALE: I think that ultimately The Greatest Awakening is the moment when we realize that being "out of control" is *the ultimate expression of being "in control."*

DR. COOPER: And why do you say that? (Pause) I'm very, very curious . . .

NEALE: What I mean is that I feel more in control of my own life when I'm *out of control* of what's going on in my exterior world than in the moments where I thought that I really had a certain level of control. Because when I'm "out of control," the level of personal control that I have is magnified, in the sense that I am controlling my individual experience so broadly that I can literally be "out of control" of day-to-day circumstances and events, and not have that condition of being "out of control" *control me.*

When I do not allow being "out of control" to control me, *I am then in ultimate control.* I get to decide what the exterior events of life mean. I become the God of my own Universe.

DR. COOPER: That makes total sense. The moment we maintain personal control, regardless of what "out of control" events are occurring around us, is the moment that nothing can then "throw us off our game." We no longer allow fear to hold us back in the creative expression of our soul's agenda.

So perhaps the greatest demonstration of control is to take a situation that appears "out of our control" and to no longer let it negatively affect our internal world.

Is that what you're saying?

NEALE: Precisely. Not only do we not let it negatively affect our internal world, we actually *cause it to be a magnificent aspect of that internal world.* We say to the part of ourselves that sees the outer world out of control: "Watch this. *Watch me control my experience of the out-of-control-ness.*"

If that isn't Divinity, I don't know what is. We are acknowledging that we have created, collaboratively, the *apparent* out-of-control-ness, producing the perfect Contextual Field within which to announce and declare, express and experience, become and fulfill the next grandest version of the greatest vision ever we held about Who We Are.

DR. COOPER: Gosh, you almost make me want to call forth "out-of-control-ness" in order to experience what you're talking about right now. It sounds almost like fun, like a challenge.

NEALE: Well, in fact, most of us do that. We're just doing it unconsciously. Why do you suppose we've created a world that seems to be out of control?

It's not that we don't have the ability to control it. With the miracles that humanity has been able to create in technology, in medicine, in science, even in certain political areas and so forth, and social areas as well, we have the ability right now to bring certain areas of our collective experience on Earth under control immediately. *It's not an accident that we're not doing that.*

It's not consciously happening, but at some unconscious level we may very well be using this device specifically as an *evolutionary tool* with which to control our expression and experience—an evolutionary driver, as futurist and visionary Barbara Marx Hubbard would view it, calling forth, *out of necessity,* our ability to know ourselves as Divine within a space that is, presumably, at the human level, very "unDivine."

It's said that necessity is the mother of invention. Yet in order for us to invent, it is necessary for us to *create necessity.* And if what we want to do is re-invent *ourselves*—or, if you please, recreate ourselves anew in the next grandest version of the greatest vision ever we held about Who We Are—we would have to collectively produce circumstances allowing us . . . indeed, *requiring us* . . . to do so.

And so, it's not a surprise to me that humanity has allowed its exterior experience in the world at large to appear to be totally out of control. Yet we are now doing this in such a way that, if we are not careful, we could lose control of our "out-of-control-ness." This is not unlike losing control of a controlled fire.

Now that doesn't mean it has to continue this way forever. I believe we're going to go to the next level soon. In the next 50 to 100 years we're going to go to the level where we allow chaos to continue to be part of our outward experience, but not at such a level that it eliminates the possibility of our outward experience *itself* continuing.

The fact that we are now allowing our deliberately, if unconsciously, created chaos to actually threaten our own ability to survive in the physical is a simple reflection of our immaturity as a species. *We don't know how to use the tool.* So, in a sense, we're like children playing with matches. And the fire we have started is threatening to get away from us.

But deeply wise and very mature species of sentient beings have learned how to contain the chaos without retaining the danger of self-annihilation as a result of it—and that's the direction in which we are headed now. Such highly evolved beings have learned the art of Creative Chaos. Not unlike a juggler, who throws plates in the air deliberately, but never drops one.

DR. COOPER: So, another question . . . something that I believe everyone reading this will want to hear your thoughts on, Neale. It may just be the most pressing question facing humanity at this time in our species' evolution. *How hopeful are you that humanity will turn things around before our planet becomes unsustainable to live on?*

NEALE: If we don't make some very important and significant and dramatic alterations and changes, it will be without question impossible for this species to continue in the ways it has been living. We're dropping plates all over the place. And it may be almost impossible for us to continue living at all in this environment. Too much broken glass.

So if necessity is the mother of invention, life as we now know it, in our present environment, will probably be dramatically changed and altered for the better in the next 40 to 50 years. Indeed, it will *have* to be, if humanity is to continue in its present expression on the Earth.

I mean, *we don't even have enough water!* They're already trying to figure out how to live in California without water. They're crying for help.

We use purified, clean water out of our taps, that has been filtered by the city, or some other system, and we wash cars with it. We take the hose and we wash down our driveway with drinking water. *And we are beginning to realize that we don't have enough drinking water to do that.*

Right now in California they recently passed a new regulation that you may not use purified water to wash down your driveway, to water your lawn, or to clean your car. *You may not use purified drinking water.* Go down to the ocean and get some salt water that you can't drink. Fair enough. But don't let us catch you using the water that people are trying to preserve to drink, because we can no longer afford to do that.

That's just one of one hundred and fifty areas of life that will really be dramatically changed in the next half century. I hold out the hope that significant changes in all of our self-defeating behaviors are possible. I observe that maturity and growth in a species are *exponential processes*. That is, they don't proceed along a 1-2-3-4-5 path, they proceed on a 2-4-8-16-32 basis, with that kind of ratio.

We could, in fact, before that fifty-year span is over—in fact, *considerably* before that span is over—reach the level of spiritual and emotional maturity to turn certain behaviors around. To stop conducting underground nuclear tests, for instance, and other activities that shift the tectonic plates such that we have earthquakes someplace every 45 hours.

I'm sitting here now in the state of Oklahoma as I'm talking to you, and the state government here made a shocking announcement two weeks ago. The people of Oklahoma, half of them, could hardly believe it. The state government publicly admitted that two things are true in Oklahoma. First, that there has been a 360 percent increase in the number of shakes, temblors, and earthquakes in Oklahoma in the past eight years. And second, that the *reason for it* is the amount of fracking and drilling that takes place in Oklahoma as we seek to harvest the oil beneath the earth.

The State Governor said, in essence, *Okay, we get it. WE are* causing *the problem.* And the government of Texas may be very close to being able to acknowledge that as well. It's just a question of what we are able to look at honestly, to acknowledge in ourselves with regard to our own behaviors.

It's one thing for the government to acknowledge it, and quite another thing for the man on the street, the average person, to admit it. Yet in the next 20 or 30 years, I think we will see an exponential increase in the maturation of our species—*such that many truths about our human behaviors will be obvious to many more of us, and most of our self-destructive behaviors may be altered before we get to that 50-year limit beyond which it might not be possible to put a halt to the destruction we have started.*

On the other hand, if some of our behaviors are not altered, life as we know it *will* disappear from the face of the Earth.

But I am very hopeful. I may not live long enough to see it, because I don't think that biogenetics is going to catch up with events fast enough to keep me alive that long (laughs). But it's okay. Maybe I'll come back as a new baby and experience a better life than we've ever had before on Earth.

DR. COOPER: So what would you say to anyone reading this who is in tune with the *Conversations with God* ideas, who wants to see these changes occur, and who believes in the potential of humanity to turn this planet around? What would you say in terms of *how one person can make a difference?*

NEALE: There's only one thing that I believe is effective and, to respond to your question, that we could do. That is to enhance and to expand the expression of the Self as a living, breathing, model of Divinity, *so gloriously that simply being Who We Are would set an example that could no longer be ignored.*

That would cause hundreds, thousands perhaps, maybe even mil-lions—*great numbers of other people*—to look at us and say, "What is it that you know that I don't know? What is it that you have that I don't have, and how can I get it? *How can I experience that?"*

And I would suggest we begin by not telling others that they're "doing it wrong"—living their lives wrong, experiencing their careers wrong, handling their health wrong, eating wrong, whatever. Because in my observation, this doesn't work. We have to *model* the behaviors we wish to encourage in others. Gandhi put this perfectly: Be the change you wish to see.

You know who was one of the greatest changers of people's indi-vidual lifestyles? Jack LaLanne. He was in such good health himself that he looked at the age of 70 and 75 and 80 as if he was 50, 55, and 60. He modeled such extraordinary understanding of what keeps the body physically healthy that everyone else went to him and said, "Okay, okay, fair enough. Tell us what you know."

And the same is true of people who have advanced themselves spiri-tually and metaphysically. The Paramahansa Yogananda's of the world. The Thich Nhat Hanh's of the world. The Pema Chödrön's of the world. The Byron Katie's and Eckhart Tolle's of the world.

Now imagine combining the two! Imagine a whole *race* of beings functioning at that level, physically and metaphysically. Do you think they would take care of the Earth on which they live any less wondrously than they care for themselves?

So the answer is not going to be, what can I do? Can I form a club, can I join an organization, can I *create* an organization or start a move-ment or give speeches or get on a soap box? Can I send petitions around, or what kind of *doingness* can I engage in to fend off this impending end-of-life-as-we-know-it scenario?

Don't get me wrong. Those can be helpful things to do to assist in awakening consciousness, both in oneself and in others. But ulti-mately, the end of life as we know it on this planet can only be averted by *beingness.* Those activities I just spoke of, those calls to action, must be directed at changing people's state of being. When that is changed, what we are *all* doing will *automatically* change.

What must change is what people *believe*. What they believe about Who They Are. What they believe about each other. What they believe about life, its purpose, and how it works. And what they believe about God. When that changes, everything changes. People's behaviors are created by their beliefs.

So I would say to all of those who are finding value in the *Conversations with God* material: choose to move through the space of Life *at such a high level of beingness* that the glory and the wonder of Who You Are and How you Behave will suddenly become deeply desirable. Then others will pay attention to you! (Not that you are being who you are being to *get them* to pay attention you. You are being what you are being to get *you* to pay attention to you! But others paying attention to the attention that you are paying to who you are and how you are behaving will just happen *automatically*.) Then you will tell them that this is who *they* are also, and how *they* can behave also. And in this you will *give people back to themselves.*

This is the invitation that *Conversations with God* has offered to all of us.

You won't have to get on any soapbox and give any speeches, or try to find any podium or place from which to share the wondrous message of who we are and why we are all here. *People will come flocking to you* because of the way you are acting, because of the way you are being, because of the way you are moving through the world. "Okay," they will say, "there's clearly something you understand that I don't understand, the understanding of which would change everything."

And, you know, it's been this way from the beginning. The people who change the world—and there have been those who have done it already. I mean, the world has changed a lot in the past several thousand years—and the people who have changed humanity's experience of itself have not done so by *doing* something, nearly as much as by *being* something. They have done so by who they were *being*.

That's true of Lao Tzu, that's true of Buddha, Moses, Christ, Mohammed, and other spiritual masters. Mary, the mother of Jesus, is surely
held up as such a Master. So are Hildegard of Bingen, Beatrice of Naza-
reth, Julian of Norwich, St. Catherine of Genoa, Saint Elizabeth, Joan
of Arc, Birgittta of Sweden, Melania the Elder and, more contemporar-
ily, H.P. Blavatsky, Annie Besant, Mother Teresa, the Dalai Lama, Mātā
Amṛtānandamayī Devī, and Mother Meera. All of their demonstrations
have been exactly the same. They have demonstrated their highest idea
of Divinity.

DR. COOPER: So it's about *being*, not *doing*. As *Communion with God*
says, "Be the light that truly lights the world."

NEALE: *This is, of course, the only reason to be alive.*

You see, We Are All One. So if we want to express and create the
maximum health—physical and metaphysical, spiritual and non-spiri-
tual, so to speak, of the "single body," of the one thing we are—the best
thing we can do is to be the healthiest *part* of that body—not run around
killing all the rest of the body, then saying "You're not doing it right."

I've learned that even in my own family, and in my own organization. I spent the first few years telling everyone around me how they're
not doing it right. "You're not thinking positively, you're not approach-
ing the problem in the most efficient and effective way, your attitude
is hurting you, blah-blah-blah." And that got me nowhere. And I finally
realized this. I realized that it was creating more negativity, actually, and
a reluctance to change on the part of other people.

So then I began to pay more attention to my own expression, and my
own experience. *And I began trying to live more fully into the messages
that I was inviting them to look more closely at.* And I would never claim
or assert that I have somehow "made it," that I have "gotten there," that
I no more demonstrate those old behaviors. Because those who know
me know better. But I have improved. I've shifted my approach, trying

more and more to *be* the change I wish to see. And others see, I think, the changes I am trying to make. And they're making them as well.

We're all here to help each other. We're all here to lead each other back home. And we don't lead by saying, "I'm doing everything right. Follow me." We lead by saying, "We all can improve. I'll go first."

DR. COOPER: I love those thoughts. I love that advice. And I'm going to start that right now. Thank you for those ideas.

NEALE: You're very welcome.

Part Two

~

QUESTIONS AND ANSWERS

This section contains questions that both of this book's authors have heard from many sources through the years. These oft-received inquiries have never been answered by both at the same time, however. Until now. Following is the result of asking each the same question, then placing their answers side-by-side, comparing their medical and spiritual points of view.

The questions here were first answered
from a medical perspective by Brit Cooper, M.D.,
and then from a spiritual perspective
by Neale Donald Walsch.

ASSISTED LIVING FACILITIES

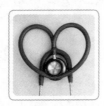

My mother is suffering from dementia. We can afford to place her in an assisted living facility, but question whether we are being selfish, or acting in her best interests.

DR. COOPER: This is a question that many people face with their aging parents, especially as modern medicine develops to the point where people begin to live longer and longer.

When we look at why assisted living facilities were created in the first place, we see that they offer numerous benefits. These types of care facilities were meant to *enhance* our relationship with our aging loved one. They have staff who can look after the basic needs of the elderly— be it food preparation, eating, bathing, toileting, exercise, medication administration, and socialization with others so that our aging parents do not begin to feel *isolated,* as so many older people do when they are no longer physically able to get out and do things during the day.

Assisted living facilities are also able to offer various levels of medical support. The nursing staff can look after things such as catheters (tubing to help with urination) among other daily tasks, and physicians visit seniors' care facilities regularly, so your mother would have easy access to medical care.

We can see that in an *ideal world*, assisted living facilities would in all likelihood be a win-win option for both you and your aging loved one. You would be able to focus on a heart-to-heart connection without having to worry about their physical needs being taken care of, nor about their overall medical care and supervision.

However, the great tragedy in many of today's assisted living facilities is that we often miss out on the gifts that elders bring. Having worked in the medical profession, and having made dozens of trips into seniors' care homes, I have seen before my own eyes much of the *sadness,* the *loneliness,* and often the sense of *isolation*—the opposite of what we were trying to achieve—occur in all too many of these facilities.

I have walked into these places and, more times than not, literally *felt,* energetically, the sense that people were *wishing they were somewhere else.* I will ask people, "Do you have any visitors coming today?" And more than half of the patients have said that they rarely get visitors . . . *not even their own family members.* And they will say point blank that they dislike being there.

So it is no surprise to me that many of them sink into a state of depression (with a staggering 44 percent rate of depression or depressive symptoms among the "institutionalized elderly"),[12] and many of them even lose the impetus or drive to socialize with those around them. Instead, all too many people recluse in their small rooms, wishing the hours and days away, and spending the final moments of their lives in a way that is far from the most meaningful.

As a society, we no longer value the presence of elders as we used to, *and to our loss.* Elders used to be deeply respected and cherished for the wisdom they offered to the human "tribe." And *Conversations with God* makes it clear in the first few chapters of Book 3 that this is how any society of highly evolved beings would live.

They would celebrate and honor their elders and, in doing so, would facilitate people finding great meaning in the final stages of their lives, *precisely because they would see themselves as essential parts of the community, valued for the gifts they bring.*

Given that this is no longer done at a cultural level, it is up to us now to look out for our loved one's best interest. *How can we do this?*

Looking at your mother's case specifically, I would suggest that if you do have the financial wherewithal to support her in an assisted living facility, and if you feel that this is the best option at this point—which it sounds like you do—then I would do it. I would perhaps start off by spending some time with her looking around at different places, so that the two of you can choose something that feels like "home" to her. (Unless, of course, her dementia is so severe that she is unable to help in the decision-making process.)

Once you have selected a new "home" for your mother, I would do my best to bring an excited and optimistic energy to the situation. Rather than feeling "guilty" (or "selfish") about it, I would release those emotions and instead spend time thinking of creative ways that you could make this "next chapter of her life" (moving into the assisted living facility) as positive as possible *for both of you.*

When it comes to the idea of being "selfish," *Conversations with God* makes it clear that we cannot give to others what we do not give to ourselves; or, to quote from Arianna Huffington's book *Thrive*, we need to "secure [our] own oxygen mask first," before we are effectively able to help others.[13] If caring for your mother on your own has become burdensome to the point that it does not feel good to you anymore—where the gift of *giving to another* becomes no longer joyful—then it is time to make a change.

Also, as you navigate this period of transition, know that it is entirely possible that your relationship with your mother could be even more meaningful when she is in an assisted living facility. For in giving yourself some breathing space, and in diminishing the work you need to do caring for her, you will then be able to "show up" in a way where you can maximize the joy and connection between the two of you, as well as with the rest of your family.

In closing, I invite you to see this transition that is occurring in both of your lives not as a *sadness* or a *let-down*, or not for that matter as a *"selfish choice,"* but rather, as an *opportunity* and a *blessing* as you continue to show your mother how much you love and care for her, even and especially as she moves into an assisted living facility.

NEALE: I have lived through this family dilemma, although at a bit of a distance. My wife's father suffered from dementia, and his symptoms became so severe, with his behavior so affected, that his wife of 50 years had no choice but to place him in a memory care facility less than two months after their golden wedding anniversary.

It was not a situation where caring for my wife's Dad on her own had become burdensome to the point where it "did not feel good" to her anymore—where "the gift of *giving to another* became no longer joyful"—it was a situation in which the gift of giving to another became no longer *possible.*

I don't think that anybody removes a loved one from their own home and places them in a care facility because the *joy* has gone out of caring for them. I observe that this happens because the *capability* of caring for them has been exceeded by the patient's needs.

As you've pointed out here doctor, one person, or even two, in the home cannot provide the ongoing, minute-to-minute care that a multi-person staff at a memory care facility is called upon to provide—and I want to add that this is a staff that, not insignificantly, *rotates* and has *time off* from attending to the continual need of the patient for highly personalized attention; a staff that also does not have a lifetime of deep personal attachment, and the resulting unremitting grief and loss, to deal with emotionally . . . which we all know can have an enormous effect on any person's energy reserves.

The loss experienced by family members of dementia and Alzheimer's patients can often exceed the loss experienced when a loved one dies. As devastating as the death of a beloved is, that experience of deep loss is not visited over and over again for weeks, months, or even years, as is the case faced by family members of someone whose memory and basic living skills are slipping away inch-by-inch right in front of them—and then, more rapidly, mile by agonizing mile.

The pain of seeing a loved one in a casket, while deeply and sadly impacting, often cannot compare to the stunning, cold-compress-on-the-chest experience of a wife or child seeing a lifelong loved one in front of them who suddenly does not know who they are. Adding to this monumental loss is that the family member in the second instance will then, eventually, have to embrace the physical departure of their loved one through death *as well*—and *knows* it. My father-in-law died in the memory care facility.

To directly respond to the question above, then . . . I believe that people who deeply love another are rarely, if ever, acting "selfishly" by moving their beloved into a care facility. On the contrary, it breaks their heart to do so. From a spiritual point of view, this is a loving thing to do if adequate care in the home is no longer possible, given the substantial risk to the well-being of the patient and to the primary caregiver as well of keeping the patient at home.

The greatest sadness in human society is that at a time when reports of memory loss conditions are reaching epidemic proportions, the cost of providing care for patients suffering from such conditions is skyrocketing along with it, rendering it more and more difficult to offer patients and their families the assistance they so desperately need, and robbing the surviving member of the family of whatever might have been set aside for their own senior years.

I cannot even begin to imagine how families that cannot afford in-home or facility-based care for their loved ones with memory loss can cope—and how their tragedy is often doubled through the impact such a situation has on the health and well-being of caregivers, many of whose lives are shortened by the impact of the stress and strain placed upon them.

What the highest expression of true spirituality calls for is the creation of a society whose members are committed to *care for each other*, and to provide care for those who need it most *when* they most need it. And while some countries and their citizens have compassionately done so (and should be honored for having made such choices), millions upon millions on Earth still have no access to modern or adequate health care.

We should not be living in a world where caring, compassionate assistance is available and offered only to those for whom it is financially within reach. No one of good conscience could agree that this speaks well for our culture and our species.

Yet there are those who say it is simply a problem of how far the world's financial resources can reach. Can humanity afford to offer health care to all who need it, regardless of ability to pay?

The answer is, of course, yes, if we simply, as a culture, shifted our priorities. Our collective governments spend more on their militaries to protect what their citizens fear losing, or don't wish to offer, than it would cost to feed, clothe, and provide health care to the entire world's population several times over. That is the mark of an enormously selfish society and an obviously primitive species.

(And no, that is not a judgment. It is a simple, but sad, observation.)

IS THERE A "SOUL LESSON" IN DEMENTIA?

What possible lesson can a person be learning when suffering from dementia? (Or, is the lesson for the caregivers?)

DR. COOPER: I do not hold the point of view that we are here on the Earth to "learn any lessons" spiritually. Rather, I agree with the way *Conversations with God* puts it . . . that we are here to *demonstrate and to create the highest version of Who We Are*, and that challenging situations (and adverse medical diagnoses) are nothing more than platforms upon which we *define ourselves.*

For example, as a caregiver for someone with dementia, do you choose to be frustrated, annoyed, and possibly even resentful for the burden it places upon you? Or, do you choose to be patient, caring, and compassionate? Do you choose to *see and to remember the best in the person*, even at moments when they forget who you are, and at moments where they perhaps act out in anger or rage?

This may sound like an obvious question, but it is a hard choice to actually *live out*, day-to-day, when someone you love appears to be completely disoriented to the world (as occurs in severe dementia). It can be especially challenging when a loved one becomes troubled and unsettled, which occurs frequently in dementia (leading to nighttime wandering, acting out, or forgetting social etiquette, due to confusion).

How can caregivers maintain a loving and compassionate attitude in such a situation? How does one not spiral downward into sadness, depression, anger, and resentment for such an overwhelming condition?

In my understanding, there is no spiritual "requirement" that we show up in any particular way—and no "soul lesson" that is mandated by the Universe for us to learn—but there *is* an *opportunity.* And we are invited to *use* this opportunity, this situation, to demonstrate our *highest* idea of Who We Are in relationship to what is occurring.

Regarding the patient—the one with the dementia—I will take a slightly different stance. I still do not believe there is a "soul lesson" to be learned, but I do believe that the medical profession could handle dementia, on the whole, differently, so as to alleviate some of the suffering that I, personally, view as unnecessary.

I believe this relates back to our discussion on euthanasia earlier in the book, and to our willingness—as physicians and as a society—to take the time to talk to people about their "goals of care" (things such as *Advance Directives*, which startlingly, only 33 percent of elderly patients in the United States have in writing)[14] prior to their mental state deteriorating to the degree that such conversations can no longer take place in a meaningful way.

I think we would be doing people a *great service* by clarifying what physical or mental conditions they are willing to live with, and which ones they are not—so that we would be able to help them end their life when their condition (physical or mental) deteriorated past this point.

I would also like to mention here that the majority of people who live long enough to get dementia (not all of them, but a great many of them) *are alive in large part thanks to western medicine.* That is, if we did not have treatments available for heart disease, diabetes, kidney disease, infections, and a whole host of other conditions, *these people likely would have passed on long before dementia struck.* (For instance, if humanity were "living in the wild" without access to medical treatments, few people would ever survive to the point of getting dementia in the first place.)

Therefore, if we, as western medical doctors, are in large part responsible for keeping people alive to the point where they then *move into dementia*, are we not also responsible for helping them to "leave," or to "exit" the physical plane, once their condition (physical or mental) has deteriorated to the point of no longer being functional? *Would this not equally be our responsibility?* (Assuming, of course, that they have stated in an *Advance Directive* that this would be their first choice.)

It was never brought up in my medical training, but it is something that has lingered in my mind from the very first nursing home visits I made, when I saw before my own eyes the struggle that so many endure as a result of dementia. And I remember thinking to myself in those moments, "My goodness, if we, as medical doctors, have brought people to this place, *is it not also our responsibility to help them on their way 'out'?"*

So I would close by saying that dementia, in my view, is a condition that humanity could handle differently. And I see those who "suffer from dementia" as providing the impetus for world change . . . or at least for the changing viewpoints of both the medical profession and the legal system around how we, as a culture, handle "terminal diagnoses."

In this way, the souls of these patients could very well be accepting an invitation *at a very high level*—being willing to stand in those shoes so that the rest of the world can awaken to a new way of doing things, and so that a new medical *protocol* for patients with terminal diagnoses such as dementia (including planning "goals of care" and the *option* for euthanasia) could come into play.

I will turn it over to you, now, Neale . . . if you have things to add from a spiritual point of view.

NEALE: I am going to say something here that is going to turn our entire understanding and experience of "dementia" upside-down.

First, I want to announce without hesitation or equivocation that the person suffering from dementia is not doing so to "learn" something—and neither is the situation occurring to allow the caregiver to learn something.

Spiritually, I have come to understand that life is not an opportunity for us to learn, but an opportunity for us to demonstrate; not an opportunity for us to DIS-cover, but an opportunity for us to UN-cover, Who We Really Are. That is, the whole of life is not a process of discovery, but of recovery—or, if you wish, of *remembering* our True Identity.

Nor is this an individual process, but one in which all souls are engaged collaboratively. We have co-created this experience we call dementia, and have done so in families and clans where the commitment to the greatest spiritual understanding is very, very high.

This is true in my wife's family. My wife Em is herself deeply committed to doing whatever it takes to advance the evolution of her soul—and to helping every human being around her do the same. I want to share with you now something that she had on more than one occasion explained to me when she came home after visiting her father when he was living in a memory care facility.

The person with dementia has let go of all prior notions of their limited physical identity. Their soul is still very much present (*very* much), but their mind has released, one by one, every idea—literally, every memory—of themselves that is confined to a single set of facts, events, or circumstances.

In a very real sense, they have become spiritually enlightened. And that is why they will often say the most enlightened, seemingly disconnected things. They also live completely in the present moment, and so to us they seem disoriented, when, in fact, they are oriented to Ultimate Reality, and to the Ever-present Moment of Now, more profoundly than people who are still living inside of their "container" are experiencing.

After hearing this from Em, it came to me that in certain ancient cultures, people who exhibited signs of what we today call dementia were treated as honored masters in the clan, waited on hand and foot, their every physical need served by the whole community with loving care, as an honor—because it was observed that these members of the tribal family had achieved release from their mind *without having to leave their body to do so.*

This was considered the ultimate demonstration of "graduation." The ultimate expression of mastery.

The sadness of modern times is that our society has completely reversed its understanding of this sacred condition, with it actually being seen by many as almost a curse, or at the very least the saddest event. Yet those who understand the true nature of the experience, as did my wife, *consciously decide* to interact with their elderly loved one *on a soul level*— and often find the most amazing messages coming from them.

These blessed elders may have let go of their limited physical identity, but they have not forgotten anything at a soul level—least of all the truth and the wonder of Love. As my wife has told me—and demonstrated every time she visited her father—simply treat them with love and you'll see them light up with the brightness of recognition. Even if they don't recognize your face, they will recognize your *essence.* They will recognize love, and in this they will surely know who you are.

Em saw clearly that this is their gift to us. This is their reminder. By showing us who *they* really are through the utter and complete release of who they are *not,* they have shown us who *we* really are.

At a time when the Earth's people could benefit from hearing this message more loudly and more dramatically than ever before, it is not surprising that cases of so-called "dementia" have reached epidemic proportions. Souls are taking on the challenge. Souls are embracing the mission. As their last act on Earth this time around, souls are accepting the ultimate assignment. We are being shown Who We Are, and who we are not, right in front of our faces.

Let those who have ears to hear, listen. What a gift our elders have given us in their final demonstration of love.

CONCERN ABOUT PRESCRIPTION MEDICATIONS

I have borderline high cholesterol and my doctor is recommending that I take statins. I fear the side effects of these drugs. What are some other options or ways I can reduce my dependence on drug therapies?

DR. COOPER: If your cholesterol is borderline high, your doctor will likely support you in a trial of *lifestyle methods* to reduce your cholesterol before asking that you start a statin medication. These include increasing your exercise, as well as modifying your diet to contain less fats, in particular saturated fats.[15]

Exercise, as we all know, has numerous benefits for the body, and it has been shown to improve cholesterol as well. In particular, aerobic exercise (things like running, walking, swimming, or riding a bike—anything that raises your heart rate for at least 20-30 minutes) promotes the formation of "good cholesterol" (HDL) as opposed to "bad cholesterol" (LDL).[15] Exercise also helps with weight loss, so for people who are overweight this is another important benefit.

Any exercise is better than no exercise (presuming you are not physically restricted from exercise in any way). A good goal to aim for is to work towards 20-30 minutes of moderate exercise at least three times per week.

When it comes to diet, the number one thing to significantly reduce if you are hoping to lower your cholesterol levels is your consumption of fats and, in particular, saturated fats.[15] The current medical guidelines suggest that no more than 30 percent of your daily calories should come from fat, and it is important to be especially attentive to this guideline for those with borderline high cholesterol.

An ideal breakdown (of your diet) would be approximately 20 percent of your calories from protein sources, 30 percent or *less* of your calories from fat sources, and 50-60 percent of your calories from carbohydrate sources (which *include fruits and vegetables*, as well as other carbohydrate sources—preferably with lower "glycemic indices," such as whole grain breads, quinoa, or rolled or steel-cut oats—as these are absorbed more slowly into your bloodstream and are better for your overall health).

With these diet and exercise strategies in mind, it may be helpful to know that most medical doctors (in Canada, anyway, where I was trained) are taught to allow the patient to try "lifestyle modifications" for about three months, and then to measure the cholesterol levels once more. At the point of reassessment, if your cholesterol levels are still high, your doctor will in all likelihood suggest the statin medication again. The reason for this is that cholesterol is an important risk factor for heart attacks and strokes, which are, of course, *medical outcomes we want to avoid.*

In addition to lifestyle changes and medications, someone reading this book might also inquire about spiritual, or alternative, methods of healing that might help to lower one's cholesterol levels. In fact, I had one such person approach me at Neale's most recent Homecoming Event (a program where he invites eight or ten people to his home over the course of five days to explore in depth the *Conversations with God* messages).

This woman approached me and said, "I've decided to quit my statin medication because I am spending more of my time doing spiritual things so I figure I don't need it anymore. What do you think, Doctor?" She did not tell me what those particular "spiritual things" were that she was doing, but I can tell you that what I said to this woman is what I would say to anyone asking me a question along these lines.

I told her that, having been trained as a medical doctor, I do not know the efficiency or effectiveness of "alternative or spiritual treatments." Do I believe they work? Of course I do. I have heard enough stories, and enough accounts from various people, of these sorts of "treatments" or "healings" having produced measurable changes for the better in people's health.

What I advised this woman to do was to continue with the treatments and healing processes of her choice, but to consider scheduling a follow-up appointment with her physician so that she could at least *know whether what she was doing was having the desired impact.* In other words, she could then have an accurate assessment (in the form of a numerical value from a blood test) as to whether or not her cholesterol levels were changing and improving as a result of the steps she was taking.

Now some people may not care; they may simply be opposed to conventional western medicine and prefer to have nothing to do with it. They may choose not to take the statin for the sole reason that they are skeptical about drugs prescribed by western medical doctors. And I have encountered more than one person with this point of view. But it is nevertheless my belief that one is well-advised to at least *consider* all possible modes of healing.

Also, if you begin the statin medication, there is nothing preventing you from stopping it down the road should you (a) develop bothersome side effects, or (b) have your cholesterol levels reassessed and find that they are low enough that you no longer need the drug.

Always know that just because you start a medication does not mean you need to stay on it forever.

NEALE: I agree with you, Brit, here on all accounts. I think that one of the healing tools that God has given our species is the knowledge of how to use substances and approaches for healing—from the earliest medicine people in our clans and tribes who learned how to use substances occurring naturally in our environment (the bark of trees, the roots of plants, etc.), to medical researchers and doctors who have learned how to create substances developed in laboratories—all toward the same end: to produce health and healing in the human body.

I do not personally subscribe to the notion that today's pharmaceuticals and 21st century medical procedures are antithetical to God's healing process. Rather, I see modern medicine as part *of* it—even as the whole world can be part of the process by which all sentient beings may use every aspect of life as a means of healing every and any False Thought they may hold about themselves. (We spoke about this in Section One of this book, when we explored the fact that our world and our lives very often seem out of control.)

Spirituality and Medicality (I just made up a great word!) are not opposite ends of a spectrum, but rather, component parts of the whole range of energy expressions of which life Itself is comprised. Thus, I think neither spirituality nor medicality are profitably dismissed out of hand.

Interestingly, spiritual messengers and medical doctors are usually the last persons to do so. It is usually a skeptical public—those who in every instance doubt the efficacy of spiritual healing and those who in every instance question the benefits of modern medicine—who issue such proclamations.

What I am saying is that modern medicine and contemporary spirituality are not juxtaposed. And let me tell you that it has been my experience and my observation that what a person believes *can* have a huge influence on what occurs in a person's life.

If, for instance, you deeply believe that you have good reason to fear the side effects of certain drugs, such as statins (and by the way, there are some side effects of certain medicines that even the medical profession warns should be paid attention to, and should be reported to your doctor immediately, at the very first sign of even a hint of such reactions), you should have a very serious discussion with your doctor to ascertain that she or he has no doubts whatsoever that a particular medicine is safe, and why. And if even then you remain convinced that there is something to fear, I would move very cautiously around taking that drug. If you don't believe in what your doctor is telling you, you're going to be energetically working against the energy of the medicine itself.

I don't happen to be one of those who believe that all allopathic physicians are in the hip pocket of the pharmaceutical industry and will repeat whatever they're told to say. My experience in life has been that the vast, vast majority of doctors are no different in terms of their integrity level than you and I, that they work hard at keeping up with the research and latest findings of the most objective medical studies they can find, spending hours of reading to make sure that they are not prescribing medication for their patients that are going to do more harm than good.

You wouldn't deliberately cheat or harm another, nor would you be so careless as to run a very high risk of seriously hurting (much less killing) another, and I have no reason to believe that your doctor is less of a good human being than you are.

(Are there some bad actors among our doctors? Of course there are. Is nearly every doctor in this group? No. Stop. Period. End of sentence.)

This does not mean that you should do anything your doctor (or anyone *else*) says. In the end, you have to listen to yourself, and to what your intuition tells you, and then peacefully go where it takes you.

ABORTION

*I was sexually assaulted and became pregnant, and I am not sure
whether to continue with the pregnancy. Is abortion okay?*

DR. COOPER: I am very sorry to hear that this happened to you, as sexual assault is the most distressing way in which any woman could become pregnant. It replaces what is typically an exciting and celebratory time in one's life with a sense of deep anger, sadness, and hurt.

It also brings up a myriad of challenging decisions: *Should I go forth with the birth? If so, do I desire to keep the baby? Is this even possible financially and time-wise given where I currently am in life? Do I want to give the baby up for adoption? Is abortion an option for me? If I choose this, will I be accepted or rejected by my work, my community, my friends, my family and loved ones?*

It is not an easy position to be in, and I can tell you that I witnessed many women face these challenging decisions first-hand in my medical training when I worked at the Women's Sexual Health Clinic in Victoria BC, Canada.

I am aware that many people object to abortion on religious or moral grounds, fervently believing that it is "wrong" to end a fetal life. Some people believe this to be true at any stage of embryonic development (that is, from the very first stages following conception); others believe it becomes applicable at a certain "stage in development" (like when the heart starts beating); and others still believe that a law against abortion should become valid when the fetus is deemed to be "viable"—meaning that the fetus is able to live independently outside of the mother's womb (somewhere around 24 weeks).

Canada currently has no official law against abortion, meaning that it can technically be done at any point during the nine months of pregnancy. However, every medical doctor I have crossed paths with in this field has set the limit at 20 weeks gestation. As a profession, most doctors feel that this gives the woman ample time to make a choice about it, while still maintaining a boundary that allows doctors to feel comfortable performing the procedure.

While I can understand the concern for fetal rights—there were protests going on *every day* outside of the Abortion Clinic (the Women's Sexual Health Clinic) where I worked for a brief period of time—I also know that my *experience first-hand with these women* opened my eyes to an entirely different way of looking at things. And it opened my heart to a deeper sense of compassion than I ever previously held with regard to this issue.

Did you know that approximately 30 percent of women in the United States have had an abortion by the age of 45?[16] So the decision to have an abortion is not uncommon.

But what I would like to comment on here is not so much whether abortion is "right" or "wrong" according to anyone's particular moral standards, but rather, I would like to draw attention *to the way we treat women and approach the issue in general.*

Regardless of one's moral standpoint on abortion, as someone in the medical profession I am acutely aware of the fact that women *need and deserve a safe place to go*—a place where they can express their deepest emotions, explore the options (including abortion) available to them if they find themselves with an unwanted pregnancy, and know that someone is there to help them on this challenging road in a *supportive, compassionate, and understanding way.*

In my view, this is what medicine is about; and, more importantly, it is what *being human* is about.

With this in mind, if I were your physician and you came to me requesting an abortion after having been sexually assaulted, *I would absolutely tell you that yes, in my opinion, this is okay.* I would also take the time to hear your story, to explore your emotions around the decision if you wished to, and to consider any other options that may be of interest to you. I would want you to feel "complete" in your decision, knowing that you went into it fully informed rather than with a sense of hesitation or doubt.

In Canada, it is expected in the medical profession that, regardless of our personal beliefs on abortion, we must facilitate our patient having access to resources and support around this decision. Even if we are not comfortable performing abortions ourselves, we must always use non-judgmental language, and refer our patient on to a doctor who *is* prepared to do the abortion and to compassionately counsel the woman around this choice.

I think these recommendations for the medical profession would serve as a good model for the general population as well; in other words, I think it would serve us well to take our own personal desires and beliefs off the table, and to allow each woman the freedom to make the choice that she believes to be the highest and best.

NEALE: Your question, "Is abortion okay"?, raises other questions: "Okay with whom? With you? With someone else who is important to you? With God? With civil law where you live?"

Let me address the spiritual aspect of this question, as I understand that aspect.

The God of my understanding has made it clear to me that there is no such thing as right and wrong; there is only what works and what does not work, given what it is you are trying to do. Your question, then, from my spiritual point of view, breaks down to this: *What is it that you are trying to do?*

Are you trying to ensure that any child you bring into the world has the very best chance for a wonderful life? Are you trying to do what is "okay" based on someone else's definitions or moral constructions, or based on your own? Are you trying to make sure you do not "anger God," or commit a terrible sin? Are you trying to move forward with your life without having your own future path and choices determined for you by circumstances over which you had no control—or to which you did not pay sufficient attention? Are you trying to respond to your own inner sense of what feels "right" for you and what most accurately represents Who You Are in this situation?

What is it you are trying to do?

If you aren't clear about this, *that* is the question I would advise you to deeply explore. And remember, there is no "right" or "wrong" answer to this question. There is only the answer you give it. You will know if it speaks *to* you *of* you the moment you hear your own answer.

With regard to God, I can tell you this: God loves you eternally and unconditionally whatever you choose regarding this or any other decision in your life. God will never make you "wrong" for anything, but will allow every step you take in every life you live to bring you closer and closer to Completion on The Journey of the Soul.

Completion is experienced whenever You and God are One *in your experience*. And this is not a One Time Thing, but may happen across many moments in many lifetimes—until it happens across so many connected moments that it becomes the Constant Expression of Who You Are.

Even then the journey will not be Complete, but will expand from there as the Joy and the Wonder of The Divine reaches out through you to touch *other* sentient beings in the universe in ways that will allow them, as well, to experience themselves as Divinity Expressed.

There's more about this matter of choice-making and "right and wrong" in my reply to the next question, below.

SEX AND DISABILITY

My husband was in a car accident two years ago that resulted in a spinal cord injury. Our marriage has suffered due to his inability to be sexually intimate. I am loyal and want to stay with him, but because this area of our relationship is lacking, I feel greatly compromised. What should I do?

DR. COOPER: Let me start off by saying that *Conversations with God* presents an unorthodox view on sex and sexuality, in the sense that it is a theology that *openly celebrates* and *encourages* joyful sexual expression. It does not suggest that sex is the one and only way to connect in a meaningful and intimate way with your partner, but it does validate and honor this aspect of our humanity in a way that few (if any) other theologies do. So I would like to start by acknowledging that it is a very legitimate concern you have, and one that I am happy you brought up here.

It seems to me that the key question becomes: how can you continue to demonstrate love and loyalty to your husband after his injury, while at the same time demonstrating *love to yourself* in honoring your desire for a sexual connection with a partner? Or, in the situation in which you find yourself, perhaps the larger question is: *is this even possible?*

If I were your doctor—and there are some doctors who specialize in the areas of sex and sexuality—I would start by asking you more about your intimate relationship with your husband. Assuming that, as you said from the outset, you value your relationship with your husband and you wish to stay with him and to work through the challenge of intimacy, I would tell you that I do believe it is possible to do so in a way that honors both partners.

There was a recent article published in the Toronto Star, one of Canada's most widely read newspapers, about "Sex and Disability." The article featured a couple, Tim and Natalie Rose, who created a Centre called the *Rose Centre for Love, Sex, and Disability.*[17] Tim is wheelchair-bound (born with cerebral palsy), and his wife, Natalie, is able-bodied. Their Centre "aims to promote the idea of seeing the positive sides of disability, particularly when it comes to love, sex, and disability."

Tim and Natalie are devoted to educating people around the topic of sex and disability, and are an uplifting and inspiring example of a couple who proudly announces that they have a passionate and fulfilling sex life, *despite the limitations placed on Tim's body, being a quadriplegic since birth.*[17] This young couple simply love each other so deeply that they have been committed to finding ways to work around the situation—despite the "hassles" of transferring Tim out of his wheelchair, figuring out positions that work, and exploring how to satisfy one another sexually in ways that are "outside the norm."

But the reason this couple went public about their sex life in Canada's most-read newspaper was not for their own recognition or fame, but rather, as a means of empowering other disabled couples, as well as to educate the general population around the idea that a fulfilling sex life is still possible for people with physical challenges.

So in response to your question, "What should I do?", first I would invite you to *maintain hope* that you can, in fact, create a fulfilling sex life with your husband. It may not be "easy," or look the same as it does for some other couples, but it nevertheless may still be possible. I say this based on what I learned from Tim and Natalie's interview, as well as from experiences I have become aware of in the medical profession of patients whose illnesses have adversely affected their sexual function.

If it is of interest to you, I would suggest that you and your husband arrange to see a physician or a sex therapist to discuss and explore possibilities of how the two of you could make some changes to more fully accommodate each other's wishes and desires.

I do not believe that an injury resulting in sexual challenge needs to be a deal-breaker or a joy-killer in a marriage; to the contrary, it may be a stepping stone to open the doors of communication and, dare I say, *the possibility of an even more loving and intimate relationship than what you both had prior to the injury.*

Both Ken Keyes Jr. and Amy Purdy used their physical disabilities as platforms into greater meaning and fulfillment in their lives (stories pulled from the first part of this book). So, too, would I venture to suggest that you may one day look back on this obstacle that you and your husband are currently facing and *see it as a gift.*

Or, in the words of Tim Rose, founder of the Rose Centre for Love, Sex, and Disability: "Let's not look at disability as a tragedy, let's look at it as something to be celebrated and have fun with."[17]

NEALE: I have a wonderful friend who was born with spina bifida. She currently offers personal coaching and teaches classes for persons she refers to as "the differently abled." When I first saw her flyers about these classes I thought, "What a remarkable way of putting it."

I agree with everything my wonderful doctor friend said above. I would put it all into one sentence: An inability to have intercourse does not equate to an inability to be sexually intimate.

We're all adults here, and we all know that there are more ways than one to experience sexual joy and its physical pleasure.

Your husband is simply differently abled. The two of you can find love, warmth, and delight in his showing you that. The good doctor has said all the rest that needs to be said about the physical aspects of this situation, above.

Now let's look at the spiritual aspects . . .

The purpose of life on Earth, as I have been given to understand it, is to recreate ourselves anew, in each golden moment of Now, in the next grandest version of the greatest vision ever we held about Who We Are. We are not our body. Our body is something we *have,* it is not something we are. We are three-part beings, made up of Body, Mind, and Soul.

If this is true, we have a new context within which to consider the question you've asked. Would the next grandest version of the greatest vision ever you held about Who You Are be a person who leaves her husband because he had an accident and his injury makes it impossible for him to have sexual intercourse?

Is Who You Are a person who adds to the tragedy of your husband's injury by expanding it to include the tragedy of losing his life partner?

Is Who You Are a person who cannot live happily without experiencing sexual intimacy in a specific and particular way?

If this is Who You Are, the way to stay loyal to your husband would be to speak the truth to him about how you define yourself in this situation, and ask for his loving help and support with your decision on what to do next in your life.

As a man, I know exactly what I would say to my wife if we were in this exact situation. I would say: "If having sexual experiences in your life in one particular way is more important to you than having me in your life, I will never stop you from leaving me. All I've ever wanted for you is your happiness and joy in life. I would do anything to help you in creating that for yourself—including releasing you from any promise you've made to me."

The God of my understanding has revealed to me that my life is not about me. It's about everyone whose life I touch, and the way in which I touch it. I believe that the highest level of spiritual understanding is reached when we realize, announce, and declare Who We Really Are

(Individuations of Divinity) and when we demonstrate why we are here on the Earth (to express and to experience our True Identity).

The soul has materialized a body and a mind in a particular way at a particular time in order to manifest a particular expression of a Singular Reality. We are the living answer to the question, "What would God do now?" That is the question I would ask myself if I were the husband in this situation—and that is equally the question you may wish to ask yourself as the wife.

And remember, there is no "right" or "wrong" answer to this question. There is only the answer that reveals you to yourself, and opens you to being the person you most earnestly seek to be. In this and in all things, it is, in the end, as Shakespeare wrote. *This above all: to thine own self be true, and it must follow, as the night the day, thou canst not then be false to any man.*

WHY DEATH OCCURS

Why do we grow old and die? I know from a spiritual perspective there is no death, but clearly on the physical plane there is death. Why?

DR. COOPER: Let's start with the medical perspective. Why do doctors believe that death occurs? Or, to rephrase that, *what, if anything, does medical science offer as an explanation for why death occurs?*

This is a question that has intrigued physicians for years. As we mentioned in Part 1, the heart has always been viewed as one of the most critical organs that keeps us alive. So initially one might think that death is when the heart stops beating. But in truth death does not occur solely because the heart stops beating.

How do we know this? Because many a person's life has been saved by CPR—cardiopulmonary resuscitation—*several minutes after their heart has stopped beating.* And the heart has been able to be restarted, with some combination of chest compressions, defibrillating shocks (when doctors put the "shock pads" on the chest and say "everyone clear!!"), and medications that are able to increase blood pressure and blood circulation and *encourage,* or *provoke,* the heart to start beating again.

Furthermore, many a person has been "saved" from a heart attack—when the heart is essentially rendered non-functional for a while, but doctors are able to go in and remove the blockage and restore circulation in a functional way *before the person dies*. So it is not the heart that is the "last domino," so to speak—the distinguishing factor between life and death.

What is it then?, doctors began to ask themselves. And the next answer suggested by the medical profession was: *the brain*.

The theory here was that, when the heart stopped beating, the brain would be starved of oxygen. Oxygen, of course, is one of the most crucial "nutrients" keeping our cells alive and, without it, our cells could not survive (it is for this reason we cannot stay underwater very long without coming up to breathe—for oxygen is essential to human life). The job of the heart is to circulate blood *precisely so that fresh oxygen from the lungs can be delivered all around the body to nourish the cells and keep them alive*. What happens in this regard, then, when the heart stops beating?

Ahhh, doctors thought, well the brain would not be getting oxygen! For the duration of time that the heart stopped beating, gradually those brain cells would become more and more starved of *the critical nutrient that keeps them alive*.

And when our brain begins to "die," we begin to lose critical aspects of who we are—our personality, our memories, and all of the brain functions that presumably (from a western medical model) *allow us to walk through the world as the person we are*.

The interesting thing about this theory involving the brain is that it was found to be *time-dependent*. That is, if we, as doctors, could restore the person's heartbeat quickly enough so that circulation could return to the brain (somewhere between four to six minutes was thought to be the "cut-off"), then the person could in fact "return to life," after being what we call clinically dead, and continue on living! So it was only those people whose brains were not receiving oxygen for four to six minutes or longer who would die . . .

So you'd think we'd found the solution! The answer to the age-old question, "Why do we have to die?" Except we hadn't . . . not entirely, anyway.

In the last chapter of Part 1 we touched on *cryopreservation*—which is the idea of freezing a human body (or brain) in hopes of "bringing it back to life" years later, when medical science has "caught up," so to speak, and "created a cure" for whatever illness the person passed away from. Well the interesting thing about this is that, when we drop the temperature of the body low enough (somewhere between -213 and -321 degrees Fahrenheit, scientists suggest), *cellular damage due to lack of oxygen does not occur.*[10]

As *Conversations with God* says (and medical science supports this as well), *life is motion.* And when we drop the temperature of the body low enough, *things essentially stop moving.* They become extraordinarily close to "frozen," and cells need very, very little oxygen (edging in on zero) to survive in this state.

And so it *appears* that if we could drop the temperature low enough, the heart could stop beating for a lot longer than four or six minutes—perhaps several hours, or several days, or even longer—and the brain would be undamaged (or at least not severely damaged) and the person could *still* be brought back to life!!

So what, then, *is* the "last domino"? Why do we have to die? And what is the answer to this question not only medically, but also *spiritually?*

Medical science does not appear to have a conclusive answer yet . . . so let's take a look at the spiritual side of things.

I believe that spiritually we die because we have come to "completion"—having accomplished what our soul came here to do in this lifetime. It may not always appear this way to other people—such as to the parents of a child who is on the verge of passing away from childhood cancer (they may very well feel *quite the opposite*)—but I resonate with what *Home with God* suggests, *which is that no soul dies at a time or in a way that is not of their choosing.*

(It may not even be clear to the *person themselves* at the time of their passing, from the limited point of view of their *mind*; however, I do believe the *soul* always has clarity, purpose, and intention with regards to when and how a person dies.)

I also believe that physical "death" allows us an opportunity *to rejoin with the Oneness that is our fundamental nature.* In other words, we can move out of the Realm of the Relative—where things appear to be "separate"—and return to the Realm of Pure Being (followed by the Realm of the Absolute), where we once again *know* and *experience* (at the moment of our passing) the feeling of being *One with everything.*

And finally, as we touched on in the last chapter of Part 1, humanity's fundamental impulse is to *continually grow, evolve, and change.* If we were to remain in one physical body forever, we would be denying this impulse and restricting ourselves at the most fundamental level.

So I believe death brings an additional gift when we begin to see it not strictly as an "ending," but also as a *beginning,* allowing us to embark on the next most glorious and exciting phase of our soul's journey—moving first through the Realm of the Spiritual and then back into the Realm of the Physical, over and over again, through the multiplicity of lifetimes we are offered.

I'll pass it on to Neale now, to expand on the spiritual part of this answer . . .

NEALE: In addition to what you've offered above, I would say that death is, spiritually speaking, an integral part of life—and so asking why death exists is like asking why life exists.

Life and death exist side-by-side, in tandem with each other, for the reason that a pendulum swings, that a planet orbits, that a solar system swirls. It's about *motion.* All of life is motion. Nothing stands still. Nothing. Take a rock and put it under high-powered magnification and all you will see are particles, *moving.*

Growing old and dying is part of the cyclical process of life itself. Everything is cyclical. *Everything.* Not only is everything *moving,* everything is moving *in a particular way.* Everything is moving in a pattern—which we can call *cycles.* This pattern is predictable and observable. It is fundamental metaphysics.

The suns of our universe "grow old" and "die." And new suns are born. Everything in existence—every single thing—"grows old and dies." Even so-called inanimate objects ultimately disintegrate, falling apart and turning to dust, given billions or trillions of years. Because it takes so *long* for certain cycles to complete themselves does not mean that a cycle is not occurring. The life cycle of a planet or a solar system may be billions or even trillions of years. The life cycle of a mayfly ranges from a *half hour* to . . . for a really *elderly* mayfly . . . one day.

We see, then, that to everything there is a season, and a time for every purpose under Heaven. A time to live and a time to die. A time to sow and a time to reap that which has been sown.

Everything in existence has a life cycle. And this cycle has been misunderstood. Notice that I have called it a *life* cycle, not a life-and-*death* cycle. And notice that I have referred to it as a life *cycle*, not a life *span.* A *span* is generally understood to have a beginning and an end. A *cycle* does not. It is not a straight line, but rather, a circle.

My metaphysical understanding is that there are no straight lines in the Universe. What may *appear* to be a straight line is simply an enormous circle, a *portion* or *section* of which is so long, it seems to not be curving at all. Its curvature is too gradual to be seen. Yet ultimately, every "straight" line has a horizon, and so its straightness appears to "end." But no "straight" line ever ends, but is finally seen for what it is: that which has no end, but merely continues in a circle.

Human life likewise *appears* to "end," and likewise does not, but merely continues its cycle. "Death" is simply a process of re-identification, through which the mind and the body understand and experience themselves to be parts of a Three-Part Being that includes and arises from the soul, which lives forever.

SPIRITUAL HEALING

You speak in this book about triggering the patient's "spiritual response mechanism" for healing. What is spiritual healing and does it really exist? When western medicine "fails me," are there spiritual things I can do to increase my chance of a cure?

DR. COOPER: To answer your question of how can one *know* whether the possibility of spiritual healing exists, I would like to divert for a moment and talk about the feeling of *falling in love*. Most of us have experienced it at least once in our lives—that feeling of being with someone and sharing such a powerful bond, such a deep-seated soul-based connection, that it defies all logical thought.

How do you *know* that you are "in love"? How do you *know* that someone is "the one"? Ask people these questions, and 99 times out of 100 they will tell you, "I don't know *how* I knew, *I just knew.*" Love is one of the strongest energies we feel in our lives, and all of us know that this is something that can be *felt* but not *measured.*

Similarly, it seems to me, are the various types of *spiritual or energetic healings.*

We can leave a Reiki energy healing, or a "de-cording" session, or receive an "energetic surgery" from John of God, and we can *feel* a difference in ourselves—in our health and wellbeing—even though this difference has not yet been measured or proven, or for that matter ever validated, in any scientific or conventional medical trials.

While I, as a medical doctor, do not *endorse* "spiritual healing" as something that can be guaranteed, counted on, or trusted to "work without fail," at the same time I do not *dismiss it.* That is, even though there is no evidence that it works in any conventional medical trials, I keep my mind open to the possibility. (With the caveat, of course, that a "cure" must be in the best interest of a person's overall Spiritual Journey, as was discussed earlier in the book . . . *and note that this is not always the case.*)

Having been trained as a western medical doctor, I will say upfront that I do not know what specific strategies alternative or spiritual healers use. So to answer the second part of your question, *What can I do to increase my chance of cure?* (assuming western medicine has done all it can and is still unable to help you), let me double back for a moment to the chapter on medical miracles in Part 1.

Here we note that *acceptance, gratitude,* and even *celebration* for the challenges (health-related or otherwise) that we face in our lives form the "energetic framework" from which any medical miracle could and possibly would come to pass. In other words, these are the basic *states of being* that facilitate such physical changes occurring . . . if they are going to occur at all.

We go on to note that one is well-advised not to *count on,* or *expect,* a miracle, however, as we do not want people to feel somehow metaphysically "wrong" for either: (a) having "attracted" the disease to themselves in the first place, or (b) being unable to "cure" it.

We also explain that, in our view, "healing" does not always equate to "curing the physical ailment." It could very well mean something else, such as easing the transition to death when a soul is ready to move on, or choosing to live with a certain physical condition or challenge in order to, at a spiritual level, most fully facilitate the gifts one has chosen to bring forth in this lifetime. And it is important to understand this distinction, because western medicine will promote the idea that "healing" and "cure" are synonymous, *when metaphysically speaking they are not.*

From a spiritual perspective, then, we invite people to *see the perfection* of whatever is occurring, knowing that, although their health condition may appear to be challenging or adversarial or "unwanted" at the surface level, when we look beyond the body and the mind and begin to *see into the perspective of the soul,* we come to see that no "healing" whatsoever *needs* to take place in order for every golden moment of Now to be absolutely perfect as it is.

If there *were* "healing" to be done, I would suggest the first and foremost thing to do would be to *heal any small or false thought ever we held about Who We Are.*

In the words of Paramahansa Yogananda, "To know God is the most important way to heal all disease—physical, mental, and spiritual"[18]—and I believe that "knowing God" is remembering that we are each Divine and that, given Who We Are, *nothing* can occur in our lives that does not serve us in some way. This does not *preclude* the possibility of physical healing or of a physical cure, but it does bring us to the place where we no longer *require* it.

So getting to the last part of your question: *what can you, as an individual, do from a spiritual or alternative medicine perspective to increase your chance of cure?*

First of all, I would be attentive to your physical health as best as you can. Make an effort to follow the prescription of Paramahansa Yogananda: "proper eating, exercise, fresh air and sunshine, hygiene, physical and mental relaxation, and conscious recharging of the Life Force."[18]

Second, make use of any other "healing resources" as it pleases you to do so, be it acupuncture, bio-energy healing, positive thinking and visualization, or whatever else you find compelling. There are countless real-life anecdotes and stories showing that these methods work and can be of great assistance to people.

Third—and perhaps most importantly of all—do not be afraid to *look within yourself.* When adversity strikes (health-related or otherwise), I invite you to get quiet inside and to tap into the resources you always have at your disposal. Listen to your own inner wisdom to the point where you once again allow yourself, as we said just a moment ago, *to heal any small or false thought you ever held about Who You Are.*

When you remember *Who You Really Are* (an aspect of Divinity who cannot be hurt or harmed in any way)—and move into *acceptance, gratitude,* and *celebration* for whatever is occurring—at this point you become metaphysically "immune" to the negative emotional effects of any so-called illness, *even if the illness itself does not disappear.*

So cure or no cure, living another ten years or living only one more day, always know that nothing—*so-called negative health outcome or otherwise*—can deny you the opportunity to express and to experience, *right here and right now, the very highest version of Who You Are.*

NEALE: "Healing" is best defined as the end of suffering. It is not necessarily the end of pain, or of a condition that causes it. The essence of healing is *seeing.* It is seeing another person or the Self in True Identity. When we see another, or ourselves, as Who We Really Are, we end all thought that something is occurring which should not be occurring. In doing so, we end all resistance to it. The ending of resistance is the beginning of healing.

Healing is not about changing any condition or circumstance, but about *changing our experience of it.* Often a dramatic shift in our internal holding of a health condition can have an effect on the external presentation of the condition itself. We must always remember this: *Energy is an Effect that affects the Effect Itself.*

Think of it as you would think of wind. Wind has an effect on wind itself. If it is a little windy outside and a stronger gust of wind comes along, the wind outside is affected by the wind that came along. We say the wind has "picked up."

In precisely the same way, the energy can shift. Only it shifts from fast to slow when it moves from agitation to peace, or from resistance to acceptance, blessing, gratitude, and celebration.

Remember this: the lower the energy vibe, the less physical and the more metaphysical is the effect. The level of solidity with which the Essential Essence is rendered physical is in direct proportion to the speed at which that Essence vibrates. The higher or faster its vibration, the more physical its manifestation. The lower or slower its vibration, the less physical and the more metaphysical (or spiritual) its manifestation.

Visualize it this way: the faster the particles of energy move, the more they create the experience of solidity. You would fall right through the floor if the particles of energy were not moving so fast that they are never in one place for more than a trillionth of a nano-second. This means they are virtually "everywhere at once," and you can't move fast enough to fall through them or get past them. Like the blades of a fan or the spokes of a bicycle wheel, they produce what appear to be solid surfaces.

Therefore, to put something firmly in place, giving it the illusion of solidity, let yourself be agitated. Watch how real things become.

Is spiritual healing possible? In my belief, absolutely. Every doctor in the world will tell you that a patient's attitude can be a huge factor in recovery, or healing. The more "at peace" a patient is about their condition (that is, the less agitated or rapid is the vibration of their energy), the more they create the space for energy to shift. It is the difference between a calm breeze and a stormy gust.

I like to think of energy as The Breath of God. It's my poetic way of conceptualizing it. And I like to think of myself as an Individuation of Divinity. Therefore, my breath is The Breath of God, and my energy is the Energy of God.

How I think—the energy I create when I think—is how I "breathe" this energy. It is what I "inhale" and "exhale." If I "take in" negative energy or "send out" negative energy, I will experience negativity.

What this comes down to is that it feels clear to me that I affect my exterior reality—with regard to health and everything else—by what I allow my mind to take in and send out. My life experience has validated this.

That having been said, resist not any exterior condition. If your exterior physical condition does not change, know that this is not what "healing" is about. As I said, healing is about changing your interior experience of your exterior condition. Seeing everything as perfect causes everything to *be* perfect, and therefore for suffering to end, for "suffering" is nothing more than an interior experience arising out of a decision that what is occurring should not be occurring. Yet suffering can be greatly reduced, if not eliminated altogether, whatever the exterior presentation of one's physical expression. Women in the moments leading up to, and including, childbirth demonstrate this every day. People in the moments leading up to, and including, death may do so also.

In truth, there is no such thing as death. All death is a giving birth.

DEFINING GOOD HEALTH

How do you define good health from both a medical and a spiritual perspective?

DR. COOPER: The body is said to be at *peak physiological functioning* in a person's twenties and, for most people, it steadily declines after that. Therefore, from a *medical perspective*, it seems to me that "good health"—or "optimal health," I should say—would be along the lines of a healthy and fit twenty-something-year-old.

By conventional medical standards, then, all symptoms of "aging" would be viewed as *strikes against our health*. So when it comes to our health, we would be fighting an uphill battle as our lives move along *even if we took excellent care of our bodies*, to say nothing of those who abused their bodies with alcohol, drugs, smoking, a poor diet, or a sedentary lifestyle, or those who are plagued by illnesses at any point in their lives.

Even though the medical profession defines such things *as "relative good health"*—such as for a "healthy" 80-year-old compared to other people in their eighties, or for a "healthy" 50-year-old compared to other people in their fifties, the medical profession's *view of health* defines it as something that, in general, *continues to decline over the course of one's life.* It is a battle that 100 percent of the time results in "failure," or death, and it is simply a race against time to see how far we can "push off" that inevitable outcome.

To me this is a very uninspiring and non-optimistic point of view on health. And although doctors themselves may bring a positive, helping attitude (those of them who have "good beside manner"), the medical profession nevertheless uses, as we have said several times now, *a crude measuring stick for health and wellness,* and one that, in my eyes, *denies the true nature of Who We Are.*

Our spiritual health and wellbeing, on the other hand, is an entirely different concept, with a much broader scope and definition.

I would describe someone who is in "optimal spiritual health" as someone who recognizes that physical life is designed primarily *to move forward the Agenda of the Soul.*

They would, in turn, carry out the activities of their life *in accordance with this agenda.* And note that this would be possible whether they are in so-called "good physical health" or not!

For instance, let's consider breast-cancer survivors "dragon-boating" down the Gorge Waterway in Victoria BC, Canada, where I'm from (this is an event that goes on regularly).[19]

These individuals may not have the best health history, and are often still at a heightened risk of relapse down the road, but a great many of them remain active in the community, raising awareness for breast cancer (the point of the dragon-boat races is to raise awareness about the disease), *and often living a life very much in tune with what matters to their soul.*

In fact, I can't count how many patients I have interviewed at the Cancer Agency whose quality of life, spiritually speaking, has actually *increased* after a presumably "devastating diagnosis," as it caused them to reconsider the *whole point of what their life is about.*

And, following the diagnosis, they then began to live in a way that *served the Agenda of their Soul,* as opposed to simply gathering the "physical accouterments" of life without paying much attention to things of deeper meaning and value.

So what is the Agenda of the Soul?, one might very well ask at this point.

The Agenda of the Soul is to bring forth the qualities within ourselves that we view as most central to our humanity and, in particular, to the highest way that we can see ourselves "showing up" in this world. *And this might look slightly different for everyone.*

For the caregiver of an aging parent with dementia, it may mean "showing up" in a way that is caring, compassionate, patient, and unconditionally loving, despite the challenges of playing such a role in another's life.

For the parent of a new baby, it may mean loving that baby so much that you sacrifice other aspects of your life in order to care for and nurture him or her during these pivotal years of growth and development.

And for a medical doctor, it may mean offering *healing* not only through the prescriptions you write, but also through your *presence* and *way of being with your patients.*

A simple way to put it would be to say that the Agenda of our Soul is to *bring forth Divine states of being.* In other words, to bring to physicality, through the gift of our current lifetime, the literal down-to-Earth, on-the-ground experience of Divinity *that could not be achieved in the Spiritual Realm alone.*

And when we begin to experience ourselves in this way, *we immediately fall in love with the feeling!* Ask anyone who has truly *tried* this way of living and they will tell you that the joy and fulfillment it brings is incomparable to almost anything else they have experienced in their life.

And there is a reason for this. It is because we are tapping into the *real reason we have come to the planet to begin with.* In other words, we are aligned with our *true purpose* (which, by the way, has nothing to do with what we are "doing" and everything to do with how we are "being" . . . a point that is explored at length in the *Conversations with God* dialogues).

When we begin to live in this way, we immediately become compelled to share it with others, in hopes that they, too, may feel the profound sense of joy and purpose that we feel. And we begin "giving people back to themselves"—a term used frequently in *Conversations with God* to mean *showing others back to the truth of Who They Are (as Divine entities having a physical experience upon the Earth),* just as we, too, have come to remember this powerful and life-changing truth about Who We Really Are.

So in this sense *everyone is a healer,* whether we have a medical degree (or some other spiritual or alternative healing credential) or not. Each of us holds the capacity to walk upon this Earth in a way that is Divine and, in doing so—as we heal our own false thoughts of who we thought we were, and step into our True and Highest Self—*we may also heal others of any false thoughts about Who They Are.*

And this summarizes what I believe it means to be *spiritually healthy, and spiritually thriving.*

So as we bring this book to a close, I invite you all—as readers—to go forth on your journey as the grandest version of the greatest vision ever you held about Who You Are. You are nothing less than Divine, and it is time that you truly *know* this about yourself.

And I invite you now to *live it*—more than you ever have before. You will find that in doing so your "spiritual health" will soar . . . and I would not be surprised if you notice improvements in your physical health and well-being as well. For the two are fundamentally linked, and your physical being is the greatest platform ever on which to bring forth the qualities of Divinity Itself.

NEALE: I think the good doctor has stated it perfectly. "Good health" is simply knowing Who You Are (an Individuation of Divinity)—and then, demonstrating that. I join in Dr. Cooper's invitation.

Blesséd be.

References

1. Amy Purdy. Featured on Oprah's *Super Soul Sunday*. Book title: *My Own Two Feet*. Published by HarperCollins in 2014. Website: http://amypurdy.com

2. Emery N. Brown, M.D., Ph.D.; Ralph Lydic, Ph.D.; and Nicholas D. Schiff, M.D. "General Anesthesia, Sleep, and Coma." *New England Journal of Medicine*, 2010, December 30: 363(27): 2638-2650.doi: 10.1056/NEJMra0808281. Available at: http://www.ncbi.nlm.nih.gov/pmc/articles/PMC3162622/

3. David R. Larach and Neville M. Gibbls. "Anesthetic Management During Cardiopulmonary Bypass." Medical Textbook: *A Practical Approach to Cardiac Anesthesia*, Chapter 7. Available at: http://tele.med.ru/book/cardiac_anesthesia/text/he/he007.htm

4. Jill Sakai. "Study reveals gene expression changes with meditation." *University of Wisconsin-Madison News*. Interview with study author Richard J. Davidson (study published in the *Journal of Psychoneuroendocrinology*). Article published December 4, 2013. Available at: http://news.wisc.edu/22370

5. Brittany Maynard. For more information around her story, visit the following website: http://thebrittanyfund.org

6. Anita Moorjani. *Dying To Be Me*. Published by Hay House in September 2014.

7. Ken Keyes, Jr. *A Handbook to Higher Consciousness*. Published in 1973 by Living Love Center.

8. Katelyn Verstraten. *Globe and Mail* article: "Kalydeco: A 'miracle drug,' with a catch." Published June 20, 2014. Available at: http://www.theglobeandmail.com/life/health-and-fitness/health/kalydeco-a-miracle-drug-with-a-catch/article19278862/?page=all

9. Diana Mehta. *Huffington Post* article: "Angelina Jolie 'Effect' Pushed More High-Risk Women To See Cancer Screenings." Published September 2, 2014. Available at: http://www.huffingtonpost.ca/2014/09/02/angelina-jolie-effect-cancer-screening_n_5755380.html

10. Information on *cryonics (cryopreservation)* available at ALCOR, a leading-edge company in this research field: http://www.alcor.org

11. David McCormack. *Mail Online* article: "'I fear death': Talk show legend Larry King, 81, wants to freeze his body when he dies so he can return one day and continue to interview people." Published March 18, 2015. Available at: http://www.dailymail.co.uk/news/article-3001550/I-fear-death-Talk-legend-Larry-King-81-wants-freeze-body-dies-return-one-day-continue-interview-people.html

12. Canadian Institute for Health Information. "Depression Among Seniors in Residential Care." Published May 20, 2010. Available at: https://secure.cihi.ca/estore/productFamily.htm?pf=PFC1432

13. Arianna Huffington. *Thrive: The Third Metric to Redefining Success and Creating a Life of Well-Being, Wisdom, and Wonder.* Published by *Harmony Books* in 2014.

14. Dan K. Morhaim, M.D., and Keisha M. Pollack, Ph.D., MPH. "End-of-Life Care Issues: A Personal, Economic, Public Policy, and Public Health Crisis." *American Journal of Public Health.* Published in 2013;103(6):e8-e10. Available at: http://www.medscape.com/view-article/805452_2

15. Catherine Anastasopoulou, M.D., Ph.D. "Polygenic Hypercholes-terolemia." *Medscape Medical Review*. Last updated July 29, 2015. Available at: http://emedicine.medscape.com/article/121424-overview

16. Guttmacher Institute Fact Sheet. "Induced Abortion in the United States." Published in July, 2014. Available at: http://www.guttmacher.org/pubs/fb_induced_abortion.html

17. Katelyn Verstraten. *Toronto Star* article: "Surprise! Disabled people have sex." Published October 5, 2014. Available at: http://www.the-star.com/news/insight/2014/10/05/surprise_disabled_people_have_sex.html

18. Paramahansa Yogananda. "Quotes on Healing." Available at: http://www.yogananda.com.au/gurus/yoganandaquotes05b.html

19. Breast Cancer Survivor Dragon Boat Team—Victoria BC, Canada. More information available at their website: http://islandbreaststrokers.com

ADDITIONAL RESOURCES

You may continue the dialogue that you have found here by going to:
www.GodandMedicine.info

As well, you may discuss and explore any aspect of the messages in *Conversations with God* at *www.CWGConnect.com*, a resource site offering an extensive array of audio, video, and written content from Neale in which he expands on the *CwG* material and its application.

About the Authors

NEALE DONALD WALSCH is a modern day spiritual messenger whose work has touched the lives of millions. He has written twenty-nine books on contemporary spirituality in the twenty years since he reported having an experience in which he felt the presence of The Divine, began writing questions to God on a yellow legal pad, and received answers in a process that he describes as exactly like taking dictation. What emerged from that encounter was the nine-part *Conversations with God* series, which has been published in every major language of the world.

Mr. Walsch has told his readers and the media—which has brought global attention to his experience—that everyone is having conversations with God all the time, and that the question is not: To whom does God talk? The question is: Who listens?

He says his whole life has been changed as a result of his own decision to listen. He took notes on the questions in his heart and the answers he was receiving, so that he would always remember his exchanges with Deity. It wasn't until later that he realized he was being invited to place these words into the world, as one of many throughout history who have made their very best effort to hear and to articulate God's messages. He knows that everyone is receiving these messages, and invites all people everywhere to both share them and live them as best they can, for Neale believes the world would change overnight if only a fraction of its people embraced God's most important message of all: *You've got me all wrong.*

DR. BRIT COOPER, M.D., is a physician and lead scientist for Continuing Medical Education, writing professional development material for physicians and specialists.

Dr. Cooper is also the author of the forthcoming book *From Doctor to Healer: A Clarion Call to the Medical Profession*. She has won numerous prestigious awards and recognitions including the Governor General's Academic Gold Medal of Canada, the Duke of Edinburgh Gold Award, and an International Young Women in Public Affairs Award for leadership and commitment to public service and civic causes.

Dr. Cooper has worked closely with Neale Donald Walsch. In Neale's words, "Dr. Brit Cooper is one of the single most brilliant people I have been gifted to know in this lifetime. Combined with her inordinate kindness, compassion, openness of heart, and deep spiritual awareness, she is a treasure for our species. Watch for this young lady's name in the years ahead. She is already touching the world in extraordinary ways."

Related Titles from Rainbow Ridge
Read more about them at *www.rainbowridgebooks.com*.

God's Message to the World: You've Got Me All Wrong
by Neale Donald Walsch

Conversations with God for Parents
by Neale Donald Walsch, Laura Lankins Farley, and Emily A. Filmore

*Consciousness: Bridging the Gap between Conventional Science
and the New Super Science of Quantum Mechanics*
by Eva Herr

Dying to Know You: Proof of God in the Near-Death Experience
by P. M. H. Atwater

Rita's World: Explanations from the Other Side
by Frank DeMarco

Messiah's Handbook: Reminders for the Advanced Soul
by Richard Bach

When the Horses Whisper
by Rosalyn Berne

Quantum Economics
by Amit Goswami

Soul Courage
by Tara-jenelle Walsch

The Secret of Effortless Being
by Ronny Hatchwell and Zach Sivan

God Within
by Patti Conklin

Liquid Luck: The Good Fortune Handbook
by Joe Gallenberger

Imagine Yourself Well
by Frank DeMarco

What to Do When You're Dead
by Sondra Sneed

The Healing Curve
by Sara Chetkin

Rainbow Ridge Books publishes spiritual, metaphysical, and self-help titles, and is distributed by Square One Publishers in Garden City Park, New York.

To contact authors and editors, peruse our titles, and see submission guidelines, please visit our website at *www.rainbowridgebooks.com*.

For orders and catalogs, please call toll-free: (877) 900-BOOK.